CHECK
WHAT
YOU ARE
CHASING

How the pursuit of health, wealth,
and self will never fulfill

CHECK WHAT YOU ARE CHASING

Chris Gardner

Chris Gardner
chris@generositydriven.com
generositydriven.com

Check What You Are Chasing, Chris Gardner—1st ed.

Purpose Built Publishing

In the spirit of generosity and service, all profits from this book will be donated to charitable causes. It is my hope that through these efforts, we can collectively make a meaningful impact in our communities and inspire others to embrace the values of giving and stewardship.

Thank you for being a part of it.

" Figuring out how to best give away money is as complex an undertaking as figuring out how to make it."

–Ray Dalio

Advance Praise for
Check What You Are Chasing

―――――――△――――――――

"I am most impressed with the ministry organization he established and operates in Arequipa, Peru. This successful ministry over many years demonstrates his depth of organization, commitment over the long term, and his zeal to help accomplish Christ's Great Commission!"

– John Pearson, Peru Mission Team Leader

"I am so pleased Chris Gardner has written this book on generosity. During the *dot-com* era, I saw massive wealth in the hands of believers that was stuffed into barns—foundations and family offices with directors and protocols and shifting procedures—and then, seemingly overnight, it was gone. Are we in an era when we once again have the resources to comprehensively capital (fund) world-changing, nation-blessing ventures? May Chris' book move our hearts in that direction."

– Brett Johnson, Author of *Repurposing Capital: 50 Principles of Faith-based Financing*, *Kingdom Economics* and others. **Co-Founder & President**, The Institute for Innovation, Integration & Impact

"Chris Gardner's vision of stewardship is refreshing and inspiring. It has given me personally, and my non-profit professionally, great encouragement to accomplish all that is before me."

– Jarod Jones, Executive Director Life Ranch

"Everyone wants a competitive advantage, but not everyone knows how to do it. Chris is an innovator, trailblazer, and well-rounded forward thinker. His guidance and leadership have given us directions regarding financial growth, sustainability, and profits. Chris is a philanthropic advisor whose wisdom in financial matters, with a focus on generosity, has been a beacon of hope for our future."

– Abby Wangombe

"Through Chris' guidance, I have transformed my approach to finances, understanding the true value of generosity and stewardship. His teachings have significantly impacted my personal and professional life, steering me towards a more fulfilling and generous lifestyle."

– Josiah Martin

"I had the privilege of reading Chris Gardner's book, *Check What You Are Chasing: How the Pursuit of Health, Wealth, and Self Will Never Fulfill,* and it is truly life-changing. As a parent, I have witnessed firsthand the impact Chris has had on so many lives, and his book reflects his genuine desire to help others.

Chris understands the true value of generosity, grace, and love, and he imparts this wisdom throughout the pages of his book.

Chris' message is both powerful and thought-provoking. He urges readers to reevaluate their pursuits of health, wealth, and self-fulfillment. His profound insights leave a lasting impression, prompting readers to focus on what truly matters in life.

I highly recommend *Check What You Are Chasing* to anyone looking for a fresh perspective on what it means to live a fulfilling and purpose-driven life. Chris has a unique ability to inspire and motivate, and his book is a testament to his unwavering commitment to making a positive difference in the world. Thank you, Chris, for sharing your wisdom and insight."

– Austin Gardner

"Chris has plumbed the depths of Scripture, laboring over each principle he discovered before he penned these words of wisdom. *Check What You Are Chasing* reminds us we cannot serve both God and money—but we CAN serve God through stewardship and generosity. His passion and perspective, based on solid study and application of Scripture, have challenged me to the core. This book will do the same for you."

– Joshua Rowe

"Working with Chris has helped me understand the importance of understanding the balance between wealth, purpose, and generosity. Through his guidance, he opened my eyes to how to give back and be more generous in an intelligent way. I'm very thankful for Chris and his professional mentorship."

– Doug Porterfield

"I've known Chris Gardner and his family for a while and he is just like his Dad. Their family are God-loving people, forgiving and willing to help. I hesitated to call Chris about our finances because it's too complicated. So I finally called him and he immediately gave me his time to talk. He showed me a vision on how to manage what I have and what I can do with my time in the future to see God's work if I can manage my finances better. We have been debt-free except for the mortgage and are able to save more money every month. He has been a blessing and encouragement to us and we appreciate his help.

Thank you for all you do, Chris."

– Faith and Lang Insisiengmay

"In Check What You Are Chasing, Chris Gardner delivers a profound exploration of wealth's true essence. As someone who lives by his principles, Chris offers invaluable firsthand wisdom that has profoundly reshaped how I prioritize my time and resources daily. His insights on stewardship and generosity are not just transformative but deeply inspiring."

– Trent Coker

"Thanks to Chris' mentorship, I've gained a profound under-standing of the intersection between financial success and meaningful living, allowing me to achieve both professional excellence and personal fulfillment.

– Blake Young

"Over the past several years that I have had the pleasure of working professionally with Chris, our family and business have been forever changed. Chris takes a Christ-centered, dynamic approach to opportunities and issues that, when mixed with his experience and plethora of uniquely effective strategies, generates a very clear and attainable path to success. The prescribed low-impact changes that produce highly impactful, positive results are founded in Scripture and promote abundant Christian living.

Serving God with our money as a steward of those resources, was a reasonably new idea, in the context as discussed in the book. The results are glaring, to say the least. This is the only way to experience fulfillment in a secular world where the dollar is the driver. I would encourage anyone looking to understand and achieve things like fulfillment, peace, and abundance, to read this book. Thoroughly absorb the principles and perspectives presented and try deploying them as soon as possible. You will not be disappointed."

– Stephen Hobbs

"Integrity, character, respect, ethics, greater purpose, selflessness....all phrases that seem to be increasingly used by certain business leaders and organizations. Too often though, they have become cliché buzzwords to cover common practices that are the very opposite of those words' meanings. Eventually, it becomes clear that the emperor has no clothes on and everyone has just been afraid to speak up and offer a better, authentic, and meaningful way of doing life and business.

Chris has a resume that shows life can be lived differently, filled with deep significance, and creating a positive impact on those around us. He takes the meaningless buzz out of the buzzwords and reveals what it means to truly pursue the greater virtues in life without sacrificing vocational and personal excellence."

– Joshua Arrington

"Chris Gardner is the personal, real-life embodiment of *Check What You Are Chasing*. His lifelong record of investing in others to help them obtain their dreams while inspiring each of us to help others based upon his example and the principles set forth in this fine work is why I can strongly recommend this book to you! Invest in yourself by diving in!"

– John Moore

"I have worked beside Chris Gardner for many years in places all over the world where he formulated, sharpened, and perfected the concepts you will find in his book, *Check What You Are Chasing: How the Pursuit of Health, Wealth and Self Will Never Fulfill*. These life-changing concepts, if put into practice, have the potential to transform your path into a more fruitful existence in the here and now and also leave a lasting legacy of true wealth to future generations. The holistic approach to life outlined in the pages of this book will give you the inside track on living a life of true generosity, which leads to a genuine satisfaction not found on other paths."

– Bruce Snead

"I have been extremely encouraged and challenged by Chris' book *Check What You Are Chasing*. It is so easy to start off chasing dreams, goals, and success, but just as easy to fall into the pitfall of selfish gain. Chris' book helps us refocus and find the balance in our wealth management and stewardship of our finances. I was encouraged to look at my wealth as a tool to advance the right thing and not for selfish desires. Understanding that our real fulfillment comes in what we give, not in what we accumulate, helps us to experience true success in life and finances. I hope as you read, that you too will be encouraged to work, save, and enjoy life, but become a giver and find your true purpose and fulfillment in life!"

– Stephen Underwood

"Working with Chris has been an absolute game-changer for me. When I first met Chris, it was always a struggle to balance financial goals with overall well-being. Chris took the time to understand my unique situation and provided personalized advice that went beyond mere financial planning. He showed me how the pursuit of health, wealth, and self could be harmonized rather than seeing them as separate or conflicting goals. Chris' wisdom and guidance have not only helped me achieve financial stability but also improved my overall quality of life. Chris' dedication to his clients is evident in every interaction. He is so much more than just a financial advisor."

– Michael Lonati Jr.

"I've known Chris for over 15 years, and in *Check What You Are Chasing*, he delivers a message that deeply resonates with me regarding understanding the balance between wealth and purpose. This book cuts through the noise and gets to the heart of what really matters, challenging our relentless pursuit of health, wealth, and self-fulfillment.

Through engaging storytelling and practical insights, Chris offers a roadmap to finding true contentment beyond the rat race. His ability to simplify complex ideas and present them in an accessible way is truly impressive. If you're feeling trapped in the endless chase for more, this book is a must-read. It provides the clarity and guidance needed to refocus on what truly brings fulfillment."

– Seth Austin

CONTENTS

Introduction

After years of hard work and struggle, you've finally done it— you're successful in your career or business, and due to your success, God has blessed you with wealth.

But after the initial excitement of your achievement wears off and you become used to life as a successful person with more than enough money, you start to wonder... "Isn't there more to life than this?"

It feels like climbing to the top of a mountain and then looking around and realizing that the view isn't anything special.

When most people reach this point, they think the answer is "more." They think, "I thought I would be happy when I bought a nice house and a nice car... But I'm not happy yet... Maybe I should earn more money to buy a nicer house, a nicer car, or a better vacation home..."

This way of thinking is human nature... But chasing "more" is like running on a treadmill–you never arrive at your destination. Your only options are to keep running or to get off the treadmill.

So it turns out that all of the old sayings are true. Money can't buy you happiness. So what now?

This book is for those with more than enough who are wondering:

- How do I align my money with my values?
- Is being wealthy compatible with being a Christian?
- If money doesn't make me happy, what will?
- What does God want me to do with my money?
- How do I discover my mission in life and live with purpose?

As a wealth manager and philanthropic strategist, I've met many Christians who were wrestling with these questions. Throughout your life, you may have heard people try to tell you that wealth and God are incompatible. But this is false—money is simply a tool to carry out God's will. Money is only evil when we love it more than we love God.

So, what does God want us to do with our money?

Focus on His purpose for our money.

Generosity is a key to finding fulfillment in wealth. When you realize that your money isn't just for your own pleasure and that it can help others and make a positive impact in the world, your financial success takes on an entirely new purpose.

Energized and fulfilled by your ability to do good in the world, you'll begin a new life of generosity. Instead of thinking, "Isn't there more to life than this?" you'll begin to experience the richness and fullness of a life dedicated to serving others.

But living a generosity-led life after years of chasing "more, more, more" can be difficult. Giving our resources away contradicts what most of the world teaches us about wealth. How do you overcome the love of money (that all humans have, like it or not)? And how do you give your money in a way that ensures it will do good in the world?

I believe that, just as you need a spending plan, an investment plan, or a retirement plan, you need a generosity plan—a strategic financial plan that helps you use your money in a way that aligns with your Christian values and amplifies your impact.

In this book, I'll show you the path to living life as a generous person. We'll examine what the Scripture tells us about generosity, wealth, and God's purpose for us. Along the way, I'll share some of my experiences as a wealth manager and philanthropic strategist helping successful Christians become generosity powerhouses.

God is calling you to be generous... Will you answer the call?

CHAPTER 1

I Thought I Would Be Happy When...

If you picked up this book, you are probably a fellow journeyman down the road that most entrepreneurs must go down...

You had the courage to start a business, but you also know what it is like to have sleepless nights worrying about how to make ends meet. You may have given up a comfortable career and a steady paycheck to pursue your dream, praying that it would all work out in the long term. As you poured your money into launching the business, you watched your savings dwindle, hoping it wouldn't hit zero before your business finally became profitable.

But with the resolve of a warrior, you pushed past your fears, knowing that starting a business was the right decision for you.

Due to your grit and determination, you made it through the initial struggle, and you were rewarded with a healthy checkbook.

Now, the questions you have today are different from the ones you had yesterday. While you used to wonder, "Will I have enough money to keep the business afloat?", you now wonder, "What do I do with all of this money?"

Your conversations have changed, too. You've likely formed relationships with other successful business owners, and from these new peers, you hear about the various ways others of your financial status are using their wealth. These conversations about new cars, brag-worthy vacations, and tech gadgets are fun, but a voice in the back of your head is wondering if these rewards of wealth are all that they're cracked up to be.

These questions about wealth aren't anything new... Humans have wrestled with them for thousands of years.

Let's travel back in time and hear how King Solomon dealt with these questions...

In the Book of Ecclesiastes, King Solomon has it all...

He's the wealthiest man who's ever walked the face of the Earth. If this was high school, you would flip to the back of the yearbook and find him listed under "Most Likely to Succeed." He's that one guy who was so popular that he was voted Prom King every year since he was a freshman. In short, he has everything the average person dreams of and even more: wealth, success, and popularity to the extreme.

But Solomon is searching for the same thing we all search for: the meaning of life.

Solomon searches for this meaning of life in all the usual places people measure their worth—by the work they do, the wealth they accumulate, the corner office with a view, the vehicle they drive, the education they gain, the pleasures they seek, and the relationships they cherish.

Yet he begins the Book of Ecclesiastes with these grim words, "All is vanity." In other words, everything is meaningless.

It's kind of hard to find meaning when the wisest man said that everything is meaningless...

Now stop there and think for a minute. I don't know about you, but if I think that what he says is true, it is astounding to me. It is breathtaking. It makes me want to ask so many questions.

How is that possible? How is it that everything is vanity? Are you saying my education is worthless? Are you saying my retirement account is empty? Are you saying that everything I have pursued all of my life is inconsequential? Just remember I am not the one saying this. This is coming from the voice of a man that had it all.

All of those amazing things Solomon has... All of his wealth, success, and popularity...

He says that it's all vanity.

Solomon is the most successful person in the eyes of the world. He has all the riches a person could want. He lifted his country's economy to the point that silver was as common as a stone (I Kings 10:27). He's popular beyond your wildest imagination.

But at the end of his life, when he's an old man who has had everything a person could ever want, he writes that all of those things are meaningless. Solomon had all the things we all dream of having—and they weren't what he thought they would be.

To get to this conclusion, Solomon spent years of his life chasing anything and everything under the sun that could make him happy and fulfilled. Picture him exploring every dark alley with a flashlight thinking, "Is this where the meaning of life is?"

Along his journey, he made piles of money, dated the most gorgeous women, drank expensive wine, collected luxury cars, stayed in five-star hotels, and tricked out his mansion with cutting-edge gadgets. MTV Cribs would have loved to have him on the show to give a tour of his luxurious home.

None of it made him happy. All of it was vanity.

Wouldn't it be good if we took Solomon's word for it instead of deciding to go down the exact same path to find the exact same answers?

One of the greatest gifts that younger generations can get from older generations is learning from their mistakes. We get the amazing gift of being able to listen to the words of Solomon, a man who had it all and found that it was vanity, so we don't have to repeat his journey.

Many successful business owners or professionals I meet are experiencing Solomon's journey. For years, these bright, ambitious people pursued their goals and made their dreams a reality. Yet despite their wealth and success, something is missing... They're not happy. They thought they would be happy when they made $1 million. Then they made $1 million and thought, "I guess I'll be happy when I make $5 million." They pursue higher numbers and bigger pleasures, but nothing does the trick. All is vanity.

> *"The arrival fallacy says we will be happy when and then we never get there."*
>
> **–Carl Richards**

It's like the picture of the donkey that keeps going forward because he thinks that one more step might just get him to the reward he seeks.

Are You Chasing Bubbles?

Have you ever seen kids play with those guns that shoot out bubbles?

When you shoot a bubble gun, everyone under the age of five runs toward the bubbles, thinking, "I can get it, I can get it, I can get it." When they touch the bubble, it pops. But they barely process this crushing disappointment before they're off to the races again, chasing a new bubble, thinking, "I can get it, I can get it, I can get it."

Adults chase bubbles, too. Have you ever fantasized about a new car you wanted, thinking about how awesome life would be if only you could get that car? When you get the car, the novelty might entertain you for a few days or even months, but after that, it doesn't make you any happier. The bubble pops. As soon as it does, you're thinking about the next bubble, whether it's a promotion at work, a fancy new watch, a luxury vacation, or anything else under the sun.

Solomon chases bubble after bubble and actually catches them throughout the twelve chapters of Ecclesiastes, and he concludes that the true meaning of life is, "Fear God and keep his commandments."

Everything else is vanity...empty, meaningless, futile...

But Solomon doesn't think money is the problem. There's nothing wrong with money. The problem is money for money's sake. Money for money's sake is vanity.

> *"There is money and then there is class. These things are not the same."*
>
> **–Caroline Randall Williams**

Money is a useful tool to make things happen in the world. But chasing money for money's sake won't make you any happier than chasing bubbles that pop as soon as you touch them.

Solomon found that money was vanity because God was absent from the center of it all. None of the earthly pleasures Solomon had were evil at the core. They just didn't make him happy because God was missing from the center.

But when you put God at the center of your life, money and success are no longer vanity. They become tools to serve God and achieve your ultimate purpose. Your bank account and your business success can actually make you content when you unite them with your purpose to serve God and obey his commandments.

In most people's minds, there's a conflict between God and business. Following God is following God, and running a business is running a business. Business is for the weekdays, and God gets almost every Sunday.

But to find true contentment in running your business, you need to integrate it with God. Just as the purpose of having a family is to love and grow others focused on God, the purpose of church and business is the exact same thing in different contexts. Later in this book, I'll show you how integrating God and business can be possible...

The Finish Line

There's an old Barbara Walters interview with Howard Hughes, who was the richest man in the world at the time of the interview.

> She asked, **"So Mr. Hughes, how much more money do you need?"**

> Howard Hughes leaned in and said, **"Just a little bit more."**

When I sit down with a new client, I like to ask, "How much is enough?" In other words, how much money do you need to be happy? I've seen wildly successful business owners look at me puzzled when I ask this question. They may have $20 million in the bank and work 80 hours a week. They couldn't spend all that money if their life depended on it... But they've never stopped to ask, "How much is enough?" because they're focused on always getting "more." When you chase "more," there's no finish line... You can run all you want, but you'll never arrive at the end of that marathon. It's an unattainable goal.

As anyone in the financial world will tell you, "Never invest in bubbles." It would be great if it was as easy as that. But how many of us look back and realize that many of the investments we have made are in exactly that. Financial planning should be driven by our internal goals and desires, not by external factors that may be out of our control or not as important in the long term as we believe them to be. Unfortunately, many in the financial world are focused on helping clients attain "more" based on external factors without connecting to the client's goals, values, and life purpose.

Most of the time, these successful people chase "more" because they think "more" will make them happy or bring them more contentment. They think, "Enough? I'll know when I'll have enough because I'll be happy." But chasing "more" until you're happy is a path that leads nowhere... It's like running on a hamster wheel. You run and run, but you never arrive anywhere. You never arrive at "enough," you never arrive at "success," and you never arrive at "happiness." You think that if you just keep running, you'll get there—but you're wrong.

Many people are afraid to stop running on the "hamster wheel" because if they do, they will lose what little success and joy they are experiencing.

> *"The one thing I have found that doesn't seem to work is to think that there is a place where you can arrive, if you are insecure about money more money will not make it better. Money is a tool for impact, always use it that way."*
>
> **–Carl Richards**

Money can't make you happy on its own. No matter how successful and wealthy you become, you'll end up like Solomon, chasing every worldly pleasure but realizing that none of it really matters. You'll wonder where the finish line is, when you can stop running and finally be content.

But "more" has no finish line. You never know when you've achieved your goal because you don't know what your goal is. Pursuing "more" is like going on an endless run with no destination. Each time you hit a milestone, you think, "I'll stop when I get just a little bit more..." But if you don't have a finish line, you're never finished... Until you drop dead and those you leave behind remember that you pursued "more" rather than a relationship with them or with Christ. Without clearly defined "enoughs," you will never know life satisfaction. You will never really be able to enjoy your family or even your own life.

You might be chuckling as you read this because you know exactly what I'm talking about. Laying in bed at night, you ask yourself the same question: "When will I feel like I have enough? When will I feel like I have succeeded? Where's the finish line?" When is there relief from the pressure?

We need to define enough for our lifestyle and enough for our lifetime. Our lifestyle is our day-to-day needs, while our lifetime is for retirement or rewiring.

I'm not talking about having a finish line for your talent, drive, or work ethic. God needs you to put all of those things to his service until the day you leave this earth. I'm talking about the ability to be content in whatever state you're in and stop chasing more of all those worldly pleasures that Solomon found to be meaningless. We need to not confuse contentment with complacency—the drive that we have to build businesses that add value to the world were given to us by God. God wants us to succeed... But he wants us to succeed on his terms, not on ours. And success on God's terms means striving to achieve more and increase the value we bring to the world while being content with the level of wealth God has blessed us with. Money is often the reward for achievement... But that doesn't mean we need to chase achievement for money's sake. Instead, we need to be content with what we have and learn to give the fruits of our achievements to others.

1 Timothy 6:6-11 says, "But godliness with contentment is great gain. For we brought nothing into this world, and it is certain we can carry nothing out. And having food and raiment let us be therewith content. But they that will be rich fall into temptation and a snare, and into many foolish and hurtful lusts, which drown men in destruction and perdition. For the love of money is the root of all evil: which while some coveted after, they have erred from the faith, and pierced themselves through with many sorrows. But thou, O man of God, flee these things; and follow after righteousness, godliness, faith, love, patience, meekness."

Money tempts us and leads to pain, often destroying families and souls. Why would you pierce yourself with so many sorrows by following the path of destruction that money leads you down? Don't follow money–follow God. God will lead you down a path of righteousness and love.

But before you can follow God down that path, you need to let go of your ever-present desire for "more."

The opposite of "more" is contentment.

But just because you're happy with what God has given you, that doesn't mean you need to stop pursuing success in your business or stop growing your wealth...

The difference is that you'll now do those things in a way that partners with God in His plans and makes you truly happy. You'll now do those things for others, not for yourself.

From Success to Significance

What's the difference between success and significance?

Success can be self-centered, while significance is about others. When we're successful, it means we have things that make us feel good about ourselves—more money, a fancy job title, a nice house, and accomplishments that feed our big egos. But when we're significant, it means that others love and respect us for what we have done to positively impact their lives.

Significance lies on the other side of contentment. Until you have contentment, you will always look for success, but you won't be able to get to significance because you can't be generous.

Generosity means giving or doing for others. Yet most of the time, we live for ourselves, chasing success and thinking, "After I'm successful, I'll be generous." We don't intend to be like Scrooge, but if we don't give, we have to face that we are.

My goal with this book is to help move you from success to significance. If you picked up this book, you're a successful individual. You have a business or career that has made you money and brought you what others would consider a lot of success. That's great—we don't want to stop that. In fact, I want you to make even more money and enjoy even more earthly success. But rather than viewing this money and success as an end in itself that's supposed to make you happy, we're going to turn this money and success into tools to help others and honor God. As you impact the world around you, success becomes significance.

Significance allows you to do incredible things...

My friend Joe was a part owner of a software company because of sacrificially doing what it took to become an owner, buying in at every opportunity and always making sure that he was living beneath his means. The company was very successful.

One day, another owner surprised Joe with good news: the company was being sold, and Joe was set to receive millions of dollars. Joe was so amazed at the number that he thought he was dreaming. When his wife got home, he told her that he had good news. "Honey, you might want to sit down for this one..."

This humble couple did well for themselves and had a nice life, but they had no idea what to do with the large sum they were about to receive.

Joe and his wife came to meet with me to discuss what to do with the money. Joe said, "Chris, I don't need any more money. What do I do?"

I asked, "How much is enough?"

He said, "I already have enough."

I asked him how much money he would need to live if the worst-case scenario happened and he somehow lost all of his income. He told me the number, and we made sure he had enough short-term, mid-term, and long-term investments and savings to be able to keep living life the way he wanted to.

I then asked, "What's enough for your family?"

We talked through how much he wanted to set aside for each of his children.

Now, with both himself and his family provided for, we still had a large pile of money left.

"So Joe," I asked, "What are we going to do with the rest?"

He told me what he wanted to do, and I asked, "Why don't we start that now?"

Joe was a cancer survivor, and a local hospital's cancer center had supported him tremendously throughout his treatment. Joe wanted to make charitable contributions to the hospital to help other cancer patients afford treatment.

Once Joe set this plan in motion, he didn't look at his gains as dollar signs. He looked at his gains as impact he could bring to cancer patients who were struggling to afford treatment. It changed the motivation behind everything he did and raised his awareness of how and why he was watching his money grow. He became generosity-driven, transformed from success to significance, and impacted others' lives.

CHAPTER 2

Isn't There More to Life Than This?

One day, Joe called me and said, "I need you to come up and see me this Friday." We lived about seven hours apart. That Friday, I drove to his house. He sat me down at his kitchen table and said, "There's something special we're going to do together today. Because you enabled me to do this."

I said, **"What are you talking about? I drove seven hours, it better be good."**

He said, **"Just you wait."** He pulled out his checkbook and wrote a check for $100,000 to the cancer center. Tears streaming down his face, he said, **"I never dreamed I'd be able to do this."**

Then, we drove to deliver the check to the cancer center. One of the doctors who treated Joe happened to be there, and Joe told her about his donation. He said, "I want you to know that I might not be alive today if it were not for you. Not only did you take care of my health, but you and your staff showed me love and kindness during the most difficult time in my life. Now,

God has blessed me, so I want to give you this to help other patients ease their financial burden for treatment."

I was so glad I made that seven-hour drive to witness that priceless moment...

Becoming Generosity Driven

Money doesn't change people. It just gives them the freedom to be who they really are, for better or worse. It is like a magnifying glass that amplifies those things good and bad that you are. If you love things, you'll use your money to buy more things. If you love others, you will impact others through what you have. If you love God, you'll use your money to perform God's will. Without an internal shift, having more money won't make you a generosity-driven person.

You need to learn how to be generosity-driven at all stages of life because being generous is an internal state that causes external behavior–giving.

When you start out in life, there's a need to use more of your income on your basic needs. You need to feed and clothe yourself, so you go out and focus on making money and taking care of yourself and your family. Generosity needs to be done no matter how much or how little you have, but when you're poor, you have less to give financially, but a generous heart will lead you to give of your other resources, such as your time and your talent. But when you become successful and make a plan to give, you no longer need to focus your income on yourself. You're free to focus your spending on helping others.

We must always be generous with the assets that we have, though our asset distribution changes over time. If you have money, give money. But if you don't have money, you can be generous with your time or talent. Money is not our only currency. Generosity is not an amount but a mindset.

The 3 phases of wealth are:

1. **Budget:** You produce more than you consume.
2. **Retirement or Rewiring of Life:** You produce more than you will consume.
3. **Impact Over Income:** You produce so that your wealth can reproduce.

The Bible commands us to give at all stages of our lives, but when we reach stage three, we're able to amplify our charitable impact and help many more people through giving.

It's Not a "Thing" Problem

Once, Joe's wife called me and said, "We've been talking about Joe getting a boat... But he won't buy it. Can you call him and tell him to just buy the boat? He won't listen to me."

I called him and said, "Hey, Joe, I heard you're looking at a boat."

He said, "I've been looking at it for six months now. I don't know if I should do it or not."

I said, "The Bible teaches us that God gives us stuff to enjoy. The problem is that we exaggerate that point and make the entirety of our lives about enjoying stuff. But Joe, you've proven that it's not all about you. I think you need to buy the boat." (1 Tim 6:17)

"Chris, it's $100,000," he said.

I said, "$100,000? With the amount of money you have, that's like me calling you and asking if I should get the McDonald's meal supersized or not."

God doesn't want us to swear off having any nice things... The point is that we need to focus on God, not on things.

Matthew 6:33 says, "Seek ye first the kingdom of God and his righteousness." But we forget the last part... "And all these things shall be added unto you."

In Matthew 6:32, God says he knows that you need things. But unlike unbelievers, you will be worshiping God, not things.

It's not a "thing" problem, it's a "focus" problem. When we're focused on things, we ignore God. When we focus on God, God will bring the things about.

In the Book of Matthew, Jesus says, "And why take ye thought for raiment? Consider the lilies of the field, how they grow; they toil not, neither do they spin: and yet I say unto you, that even Solomon in all his glory was not arrayed like one of these. Wherefore, if God so clothes the grass of the field, which today is, and tomorrow is cast into the oven, shall he not much more clothe you, O ye of little faith? Therefore take no thought, saying, 'What will we eat?' or 'What will we drink?' or 'Wherewithal shall we be clothed?' (For after all these things do the Gentiles seek:) for your heavenly Father knoweth that ye have need of all these things. But seek ye first the kingdom of God, and his righteousness; and all these things shall be added unto you. Take therefore no thought for the morrow: for the morrow shall take thought for the things of itself. Sufficient unto the day is the evil thereof." (Matt 6:25-34)

When you focus on God, your needs and even your wants will be provided for. But they're the byproduct of the more rewarding and fulfilling life of following God and his design for the money he has allowed you to make—they're not the product or focus of life. They're the fruit of the tree, and the tree is seeking God.

1 Corinthians 2:9 says, "But as it is written, eye hath not seen, nor ear heard, neither have entered into the heart of man, the things which God hath prepared for them that love him."

The fruit that my blood, sweat, and tears produce as I chase worldly success can't compare to what God can add to my life when I turn my eyes from me to him. When I look to him and desire to please him, he pours out blessings I don't even have room to accept.

Happiness is a byproduct of following God. It's not something we can chase and obtain on our own.

How do you know if you're rich?

Nobody thinks they're rich. Because we chase "more," we tend to look at those who have more than us and think of them as "rich people." But when we stop looking for "more," we can gain some perspective.

Are you on the "Global Rich List"? Visit https://howrichami.givingwhatwecan.org/how-rich-am-i and insert your household income to see what percentile of rich you are. In America, we often lose perspective on just how rich we are as a country compared to other places around the world. For example, the median household income in 2021 for the state of Georgia was just under $67k. On the above chart, the after-tax value per family still puts them in the top 15% of the world.

Recognizing where we fall in the ranking of "rich" people in the world helps us stop chasing more and be grateful for what we have.

The Problem With Excess Fruit

Let's take a look at Psalm 1...

> *Blessed is the man that walketh not in the counsel of the ungodly, nor standeth in the way of sinners, nor sitteth in the seat of the scornful.*

> *But his delight is in the law of the Lord; and in his law doth he meditate day and night.*

And he shall be like a tree planted by the rivers of water, that bringeth forth his fruit in his season; his leaf also shall not wither; and whatsoever he doeth shall prosper.

The ungodly are not so: but are like the chaff which the wind driveth away.

Therefore the ungodly shall not stand in the judgment, nor sinners in the congregation of the righteous.

For the Lord knoweth the way of the righteous: but the way of the ungodly shall perish.

Think for a moment about what life could be like if these three verses are true.

Happiness always seems to be just a few steps away... We all have a list of things that would be required for us to be happy: "If only I could make this much money... If only I could live in this house... If only I could get out of debt... If only I could get married... If only I could get married to this person... If only I hadn't married this person..." The pathway to happiness is littered with a multitude of "if onlys." They continue to change and happiness seems to always be just out of reach. We're looking for happiness, but happiness is never found in a direct pursuit. It is a byproduct of another pursuit—the pursuit of God.

I used to preach in a city called Mandor, Peru. To get there, I had to take a 14-hour bus ride to the city of Cuzco and then a 9-hour train ride to the city of Quillabama. I would go there for a week at a time, and from there, I would go to Mandor. To get there, you had to walk two or three hours down a train track. Along the train track, there were mango trees, and if you were there at the wrong time of year, it would reek because all of the mangos had fallen and rotted.

A successful business is like a mango tree that's constantly producing fruit. The owner thinks, "I can't eat all of these mangoes." The mangoes sit on the ground and rot.

In my work, I see this happen every day. I talk to business owners who feel like all they're doing now is collecting paper. They have more than they will ever spend and more than their family will ever need, but they still work more hours than they should and spend less time with their family than they should. The money truly has no purpose except to feed the IRS when they die—it's rotten fruit on the ground.

But when you focus on God, you understand that the fruit is not for you. It's the result of the talents God gave you.

You're at the point right now where you realize the fruit you're producing is not fruit that you can use anymore. What can we do to ensure this fruit impacts others and doesn't end up rotting on the ground? Fruit that's not used correctly just stinks. Fruit is meant to be given to those who need it, and it's up to the people of God to distribute it.

To transform from success to significance, you need to consider the fact that your fruit isn't yours in the first place. It is God's. While it is meant to feed you, it is also meant to feed others.

When you give your fruit to others as God intended you to, you can have a meaningful impact on the world and live out the purpose God created you for.

CHAPTER 3

How Much Is Enough?

"We always pay dearly for chasing after what is cheap."
— Aleksandr Solzhenitsyn

Do you love money?

To check if you do, we can perform the "two-finger test."

Put two fingers on your neck and feel for a pulse. Do you have a heartbeat? Congratulations, you struggle from time to time with the love of money.

The love of money is a universal struggle that all humans have to battle with. It could be that you love what it gets you, or it could be that having a large amount of money fills you with pride.

> *"Don't forget that Jesus gave his money to the thief to be able to manage it. That ought to tell you how much value your money really has."*
>
> **—Bryce Roberts**

To fight the love of money, we need to shift from "more" to "enough." We need to set a finish line for your money so you know exactly how much you need and can use the excess to further the purpose that God has given you in life.

If we are not careful, we will find ourselves struggling over collecting paper instead of carving out purpose. Once we have enough money, all we are doing is collecting paper.

To figure out what your "finish line" is and begin to build a generosity plan, we can ask three questions:

1) How much is enough?

If all other income stopped, how much money would you need to continue living the way you feel you need to live now?

> *"The concept of enough is crazy because enough is not a number, enough is not a destination, enough is not a place where you can arrive. Enough is what you have to be."*
> —**Carl Richards**

All finish lines are not equal. There is no prescription to know how much to live on. It is something that will demand prayer, thought, an accountability partner, and much meditation to know what God has for you.

Lifestyle creep will creep up to whatever your income is and more. Americans tend to spend 1.05 of every dollar they have, thinking that they will be able to pay off today's desires with tomorrow's dollars. As you can afford nicer things, you'll become used to these things and long for even nicer ones. If you make $200,000, it's easy to think, "If only I made $250,000." Lifestyle creep can consume every dollar you make, and that magic word "more" will ensure that no amount is ever enough.

When I think of enough, I think of an elderly gentleman I know. He is worth nearly $100,000,000 but continues to live on $100,000 or less. He knows that he has enough. He has found his lifestyle, but what will he do with the remainder? Sadly, he finds himself with advisors who profess to be Christians yet tell him to save it all until he dies, then give it away.

One of his greatest joys in life is giving, yet these advisors are stealing this joy from him by telling him to wait until he is dead and can't enjoy the gift of giving that God gave him. God gave him money to richly enjoy, but he also commanded him to be a giver and to do good works with what God gave him. He is to be rich not only in money but in good works. We know he wants to give, but money managers want to store it up and steal the joy of giving from the man God blessed to give. (I Timothy 6:17-18)

"Enough" keeps the "more" away. When we define "enough," it gives us an ending point so we can avoid lifestyle creep and instead use excess dollars to impact the world. I think it is imperative to find a financial planner who understands this idea and won't just push you to chase more.

You will be very blessed to find a financial planner who has a finish line himself.

This will make sure that decisions and conversations about your finances are not driven by the planner's self-interest, since this is more than just a philosophical idea for him.

> *"If the question is how much, the answer will always be more."*
> **–Bryce Roberts**

Enough means learning to be content with what we have. God wants believers to keep our lives free from the love of money because we have a relationship with him. He is our helper. We need not fear people, the market, the economy, or others because He is for us. (Heb 13:5–6)

Believers are to be careful with evil desires, greed, and covetousness because God considers them idolatry. (Colossians 3:5)

Proverbs 30: 8-9 says, "Remove far from me vanity and lies: Give me neither poverty nor riches; feed me with food convenient for me: lest I be full, and deny thee, and say, who is the Lord? Or lest I be poor, and steal, and take the name of my God in vain."

How do you determine what is enough? God wants you to enjoy life. He came to give you life and help you live more abundantly. He loves to see you enjoying His gifts, but he just wants you to love him more than the gifts. He wants you to find that he is enough.

Here are some questions to ask yourself to find your "enough" point:

- How much do you need to live with a God-honoring comfort?
- How much do you need to take care of your family?
- How much money do you need to move from your career to your calling?

As a follower of God, you can still have a career, but the purpose of your career is to help you honor God by using your talents to create wealth. Once you've created enough wealth to live with comfort and take care of your family, you can focus on using the surplus to help others. No matter what your career is, as a follower of God, you have a full-time job as a giver.

Andrew Carnegie, a prominent industrialist and philanthropist in the late 19th and early 20th centuries, had strong views on the responsibility of the wealthy to give away their fortunes for the greater good. One of his most famous statements on this matter is expressed in his essay "The Gospel of Wealth," which he published in 1889.

In "The Gospel of Wealth," Carnegie argued that individuals who amass great wealth have a moral obligation to use their riches to benefit society. He stated that it is not only acceptable but also desirable for the wealthy to distribute their wealth during their lifetimes for the improvement of education, culture, and the well-being of their fellow citizens. Carnegie believed in philanthropy as a means of addressing societal issues and promoting the general welfare.

A key excerpt from Carnegie's essay reflects his perspective on giving away money:

> *"The man who dies thus rich dies disgraced. Such, in my opinion, is the true Gospel concerning Wealth, obedience to which is destined someday to solve the problem of the Rich and the Poor, and to bring 'Peace on earth, among men Good-Will.'"*

Carnegie himself became a leading philanthropist, donating a substantial portion of his wealth to causes such as education, libraries, and scientific research. His ideas on philanthropy and wealth distribution continue to be influential in discussions about the responsibilities of the affluent in society.

2) How much is enough for your family?

Rather than giving your kids more than "enough," we'll set a finish line for how much you want to give them and make a plan to use the excess money with purpose.

The answer to "How much should I give my kids?" is: how much have you taught them to handle? The real question is not about how much we will give them but how much we have prepared and trained them to use money to serve God. Have you taught your children to worship things or to worship God? If you haven't taught your kids about the importance of giving, the money you leave them may be used selfishly.

Will the amount of money you're leaving to your kids draw them closer to God or lure them further away? It's usually best to leave your kids enough money to give them a head start in pursuing their goals, but not so much money that they don't have to work. Some people say, "I want to give them a leg up, not two legs up on the couch." Leaving your kids so much money that they can coast on it and never learn to provide for themselves will only hurt them and their children in the long run.

3) What are we doing with the rest and why don't we start that now?

It's rare to find a financial professional who would talk about taking money out of their business for the purposes of God's kingdom.

But the truth of the matter is that there are needs today, and it's time today to start giving away the money that God has blessed you with. Giving is enjoyed as much by the giver as by the receiver, so it's better to enjoy this experience while you're still breathing.

If you haven't defined "enough" and you have an excess, you rob yourself of the experience of giving if you wait until you're dead for your estate to deal with it. But it is not extremely easy; this will take work. As a matter of fact, Ray Dalio in his book *Principles* says:

> *"Figuring out how to best give away money is as complex an undertaking as figuring out how to make it."*
>
> **–Ray Dalio**

Finding "Enough"

As an advisor, I don't judge anyone's definition of "enough." A client with no kids once told me his "enough" was $500,000. This doesn't bother me, and I didn't try to get him to move his line. But I've found that most of the time, clients will change their definition of "enough" over time simply because they've changed their focus to God and find it more enjoyable to give rather than to buy one more nice thing. It is always a game of what has more value, and once people enjoy the value of giving, it is hard for them to justify or even desire more constantly.

The point of defining "enough" isn't to limit your lifestyle and make you sacrifice things that you enjoy, like taking vacations or living in a nice house. But once you know how much money you need to afford the pleasures you want to enjoy, you can invest the excess in others instead of pursuing ways to make your lifestyle even better.

"Enough" isn't about the number. It's about changing your focus from pursuing more to pursuing God. Whether your number is $3 million or $30,000, it doesn't matter as long as your focus is on God.

So how do you find your "enough?"

Pray.

You need to download your plan from God. You need to pray about how much is "enough." My job is to make sure that, whatever you download from God, we have a structure in place to take you to the finish line.

If a client is struggling to discern what "enough" is, I often tell them to write the number on a piece of paper, put it on their bedside table, and every night before bed, ask, "God, is that the right number?"

Sometimes, people come back to me as martyrs, with a number that's too low for their current lifestyle needs and a desire to live like Mother Teresa. But God doesn't need you to sacrifice your Fruit Loops for off-brand cereal to save $2 so you can give it away. If that's what he tells you to do, by all means, do it. But God gave you money so that you could enjoy it and live in a reasonable amount of comfort.

You're a steward of your money. 100% of your money belongs to God. Both the percent of that money you give and the percent of that money you keep for yourself should be spent under the direction of what God tells you to do with it.

Sometimes "enough" goes up, and sometimes, it goes down.

I recommend that my clients have a meeting each year to discuss what will be enough that year (if anyone has ever had children in sports, they will understand why this matters...)

But "enough" is rooted in how much you need to have to live the life you want. Meanwhile, "more" is always a moving target. It's like trying to sail to the horizon.

A person pursuing "more" is like a donkey with a carrot dangling right in front of him. He's just dumb enough to keep going. We all do the same thing... We always look for more... A bigger house, a nicer car, more money...

But when you set your affection on things above, not on things of this earth, incredible things begin to happen. (Colossians 3:1-2)

How Much Is Enough?

> *"Charge them that are rich in this world, that they be not highminded, nor trust in uncertain riches, but in the living God, who giveth us richly all things to enjoy; That they do good, that they be rich in good works, ready to distribute, willing to communicate; Laying up in store for themselves a good foundation against the time to come, that they may lay hold on eternal life."*
>
> —1 Ti 6:17–19.

Using that three-legged stool as a symbol of retirement planning, I don't feel right asking God to hold up the stool if I haven't made an effort to put on a leg or two. Yet I also don't feel right taking everything into my own hands, leaving no material needs for God to provide and no need for me to trust him or pray for his provision in the future. How can we meaningfully pray, "Give us this day our daily bread," when we own the bakery?

Many financial counselors would tell me I'm not laying up nearly enough for retirement. But when I read Scripture, I wonder if

I'm laying up too much. I live in this tension and I suppose it will never be resolved. But I also know that whatever posture I take with financial planning, I must leave room—a great deal of room—for God. It's him, not a retirement fund, in whom I should trust.

The rich fool took matters into his own hands. He planned for his retirement but not his walk with God. He never consulted with the Creator of the universe as to what he should do with his money for the rest of his life. I don't want to be a poor fool by not planning for the future. But I also don't want to be a rich fool by overplanning for it. Above all, I want to make plans for the right future, the eternal one. I want to ask how each investment will be paying off not just thirty years from now, but thirty million years from now.

Many of us have accumulated not only financial reserves but also valuable possessions. At any time, not only our savings but also our other material assets should be considered fair game for divine distribution. We should be especially quick to evaluate luxury items. Antiques, art, coins, and other collections may be of great (but only temporary) financial worth. They could be used for strategic purposes in the kingdom of God— but not when they're lying in a safe, behind a locked display, or hanging on a wall.

Is God calling us to liquidate some of these items and invest them in his kingdom? Are we willing to seek his will in diligent prayer and biblical meditation? If anything we have is off-limits to God, if it's not fair game for prayerful dialogue, then let's be honest about it—we aren't stewards, we're embezzlers. We aren't serving God, we're playing God. If we consider "our" retirement funds off-limits to God, we're acting as owners, not stewards. When we ask God's direction for our lives, we need to lay everything on the table.

Charles Spurgeon writes:

> "Christians often look to man for help and counsel, and mar the noble simplicity of their reliance upon their God. . . . If you cannot trust God for temporals, how dare you trust Him for spirituals? Can you trust Him for your soul's redemption, and not rely upon Him for a few lesser mercies? Is not God enough for thy need, or is His all-sufficiency too narrow for thy wants? . . . Is His heart faint? Is His arm weary? If so, seek another God; but if He be infinite, omnipotent, faithful, true, and all-wise, why gaddest thou abroad so much to seek another confidence? Why dost thou rake the earth to find another foundation, when this is strong enough to bear all the weight which thou canst ever build thereon? . . . Let the sandy foundations of terrestrial trust be the choice of fools, but do thou, like one who foresees the storm, build for thyself an abiding place upon the Rock of Ages."

Is saving large amounts of money for retirement as essential as we're constantly told? Reading 2 Corinthians 8:3-15, can you pick up a hint about the need or the wisdom of saving up money for retirement? The Macedonian Christians had virtually no material things, yet they gave beyond their means to the point of leaving themselves impoverished. If they didn't need to think of tomorrow, why do we—with all our material wealth—need to be so concerned about storing up earthly treasures for thirty years from now?

How much retirement savings is enough? Once again, we must consider the available alternatives to invest in eternity. It's not an overstatement to say that if even one-fourth of the funds tied up today in the retirement programs of all Christians were made available to churches and Christian ministries, world missions could be propelled forward in unprecedented ways. This isn't just because of the value of the money, but because along with the giving of such treasure would go the giving of hearts and the corresponding prayer and commitment that God could use to reach the world.

Society in general (and financial advisors in particular) appeals constantly to our fears and insecurities. One wealthy widow told me of several friends whose husbands also have died who are sitting on large fortunes. She said, "Whenever we discuss whether we should give more, before you know it we get into the 'bag lady syndrome'—talking as if unless we have millions stashed away, we're going to end up out on the streets." Ironically, giving isn't a cause for insecurity but a cure for it, because it turns our hearts toward the only One worthy of complete trust, and it fulfills the conditions of seeking first his kingdom so that we can depend on him to provide for us materially as well (Matthew 6:33).

How much is too much? I can't answer the question for you. I have a hard enough time trying to figure it out for myself. But I do know that each of us should ask ourselves the question. We should also shut out the distracting noises of the world, tune our ears to God's Word, and quietly listen for his answer. We should listen to the voices that bring a balance of biblical principles, not to those who blindly follow the lead of popular culture rather than taking a serious look at what the Bible teaches.

Retirement from What and for What?

Where did we get our concepts about retirement? What do we read in Scripture about saving up for retirement? Try doing a Bible study on the subject—I guarantee you, it won't take long! How many people in other places and times in history have been able to even consider the option of retirement or of saving up money to last twenty-plus years? Typically, we see financial planning from a cultural perspective, not a biblical one.

When it comes to the "retirement dream," we must ask, "Whose dream is it?" It may be the American dream—but is it God's? For some people, retirement has replaced the return of Christ as the "blessed hope," the major future event that we anticipate.

When a man retires at sixty-five, studies show his chances of having a fatal heart attack immediately double. Our minds and bodies weren't made for an arbitrary day of shutdown. Nowhere in Scripture do we see God calling healthy people to stop working. Of course, it's perfectly legitimate to work without pay. It's your option to give labor to ministry and volunteer work rather than to your present job. But as long as God has us in this world, he has work for us to do. The hours may be shorter, the work different, the pay lower or nonexistent. But he doesn't want us to take still-productive minds and bodies and permanently lay them on a beach, lose them on a golf course, or lock them in a dark living room watching game shows.

If you've saved for retirement and no longer need to work for pay, then work for God, the church, the poor, or underprivileged children. And don't forget the great opportunity you have to become a self-supported missionary for two, five, ten, or twenty years. If you're still here, God isn't done with you. In fact, your most fruitful years of ministry may be ahead. That's true whether you're in a retirement home or anywhere else. God has a unique ministry for you here and now. Don't kill time, any more than you would burn money. Instead, invest it in eternity.

160 Charles Spurgeon, *Morning and Evening* (New Kensington, Pa.: Whitaker House, 2001): March 7, evening.

Randy Alcorn, *Money, Possessions, and Eternity* (Carol Stream, IL: Tyndale House Publishers, 2011).

CHAPTER 4

Gratitude

As we covered in the last chapter, if you have a pulse, you have a constant battle with the love of money.

I used to think only wealthy people dealt with this love of money thing... When I heard people preach about money, I would think, "Yeah, those greedy rich people need to hear that." But both the rich and the poor suffer from the love of money...

The rich person loves money, and his desire is shown in his desire to protect it. The poor person's love for money is shown in his desire to obtain it.

There's no escaping the love of money, no matter how much or how little you have. It's a struggle we all have to overcome.

And for those of us living in the United States and other wealthy countries, it's helpful for us to remember just how wealthy we all are compared to the rest of the world. Even if we feel we have less than our neighbors, we're wealthy beyond the wildest dreams of most of the world.

Imagine for a moment that you're sitting down to have dinner with an ancient king. He says, "I'm the wealthiest man in the land. This fish I'm eating was delivered to me from the Pacific Ocean. I have an army of men who run from spot to spot and hand off the fish to the next person. Finally, the fish reaches my castle and the servants prepare it."

As the king is bragging, you think, "If only he knew about Amazon..."

Today, even poor or middle-class people in America live like kings. You could go down to Red Lobster and have a fish dinner delivered and prepared for you just like this king describes, and a meal like this is accessible to almost everyone.

Every meal you have in a restaurant requires farmers, food manufacturers, logistics managers, transportation, grocery store workers, chefs, kitchen support staff, waiters, dishwashers, waste management, and more...

Think about how many people serve you on a daily basis. For every item you use in a day, hundreds of people had to put in labor to manufacture the item and deliver it to a store or your home.

You may not see all of these people, but you have more servants than any ancient emperor.

Our definition of wealth as a society has shifted as we collectively pursue "more, more, more." As a result, the average person today lives like a king and doesn't even realize it.

Imagine talking to a cowboy in the Old West about the Pony Express. In disbelief, he says, "Look at this letter in my hand. I got this delivered from Georgia to California in just thirteen days. Isn't that incredible?"

How will he react when you say, "When I'm riding in the back of a car on a road trip, I can use this little device in my pocket to send a signal 5,000 miles into the sky so it can come back down 5,000 miles and hit the person in the seat in front of me so we can laugh at the same video"?

Realizing how wealthy our society is today doesn't mean we shouldn't take advantage of those things... I'm not saying you need to throw away your smartphone and start delivering letters on a pony... But we need to appreciate how good we have it and be grateful to God for all of these incredible blessings.

The Antidote

Gratitude is the first antidote to the love of money. Gratitude is what allows you to be generosity-driven.

The love of money comes down to the desire to always have more. To put your focus and your faith in "more". As a result... We never arrive at the point of contentment, so we're never able to be thankful for what we have. Do you want to be characterized by a love of what you don't have yet?

The only way to break free of the love of money is by saying, "What am I thankful for?"

Gratitude changes our focus from how to advance our wealth to being thankful for where we're at. When you thank God for where you're at, it puts a chokehold on the love of money. If I'm sitting here thinking, "I have a problem here at my house. I have a driveway that my cars stay parked in because, in America, we don't use our garages for cars. We use our garages to store all the junk we can't fit in our house anymore. Once it gets so bad we can't fit it in the garage anymore, we go out and pay for extra storage space to put the stuff that we'll probably never use again. But it's inconvenient because I have four cars in my driveway, so when I want to go to the store, I have to ask my wife and kids to move the other cars..." Instead of looking at this situation and thinking, "Oh, poor me, I have too many cars and it's annoying to move them," I need to be thinking, "Wow, I'm so thankful I live in a place where having a car at all is the norm."

How often do we say things like, "Life is so rough for me right now. I walked outside today and tried to open my automatic garage door, and it didn't open, so I had to fix it. Then, I got in my car and the air conditioner didn't work"? If a person living in a less wealthy country around the world heard you say that, they might say, "Wait... You have air conditioning in your car?"

When I was a young man, I worked as a translator from English to Spanish on mission trips. On a trip to Peru, my friend, a young football player, was speaking at a youth conference to a room of about a thousand young Peruvians. I was translating his message. He walked up to the podium. In his message, he discussed how he liked to test stuff out before he bought it. He said, "For example, when you buy your first car..." As he launched into this example, I quickly realized that though the room was filled with a thousand people, there were only three cars outside, and one of them belonged to the American missionaries. In America, we were so used to the rite of passage of buying your first car while still in our teens that we didn't realize that the people we were preaching to were too poor to buy cars and couldn't relate to this example. On the spot, I decided to translate the example to be about buying shoes. It was a humbling moment that made me realize how grateful I should be for what I had grown up with.

Most of the time, we as human beings are so caught up with ourselves that we think what we have is the norm and that we deserve it. But we never realize that what we have is an immense blessing that most people never receive.

You need to be grateful no matter where you're at, whether you're Elon Musk, the poorest of the poor, or somewhere in between. In Peru, the average salary is $600 a month. We would remind them that in Ghana, the average salary is $100 a year... Poor as the Peruvians are, they can still practice gratitude and appreciate the blessings they have relative to others in the world who have it worse.

Most people are unable to be grateful because they're focused on "more" for themselves. They think, "If *only* I made $200,000 a year." When they reach that number, they don't even take a moment to be grateful for reaching it before they think, "Now if I could only make $300,000 a year..." We never "arrive" at a point where we can stop and be grateful because we're constantly in motion, moving toward the infinite finish line of "more."

You can only have gratitude when you stop chasing "more" and stop to appreciate how blessed you are. Our perception of reality must change.

"Don't forget the days when you prayed for what you have now."

One of the biggest changes that happens when young missionaries go overseas is their perception of reality. In Peru, we would take youth missionary groups to a landfill that people were living in. Some of these American kids were from the poorest parts of our country, lived in trailers, and received donations to be able to go on the trip in the first place. Yet despite being considered poor in America, they had TVs, an Xbox, and air conditioning in their homes. These kids experienced a shift in perspective and were grateful for what they had.

The Genetic Lottery

In this country, it's very easy to take pride in your successes. You may think, "Good for me, I've been so successful at building this business." You may have talent, smarts, and a strong work ethic, but never forget that one of the reasons that you have what you have is because you won the genetic lottery. You were born into a wealthy country where those with talent and ambition can easily find success. But if you were born in an impoverished country, would you be able to accomplish the same things?

Without the same access to food, shelter, and education that you were fortunate enough to have growing up, would you be able to be successful? Remember that everything you have, even those things you have worked for, is a blessing from God. When you realize how much he's already given you, it becomes easier to stop looking for "more" and start saying thank you for what you have.

In the Bible, King Nebuchadnezzar brags about his power and success, walking through his palace saying, "Is not this the great Babylon I have built, by my mighty power and for the glory of my majesty?"

God punishes Nebuchadnezzar for his pride by making him go mad for seven days, eating grass like a cow. He wants Nebuchadnezzar to understand who really brought about his success... Nebuchadnezzar had simply won the genetic lottery and was born a king. He needed to be grateful to God for what he had.

Recognizing you've won the "genetic lottery" doesn't mean you need to feel guilty about this. You're successful, and you've taken advantage of your skills and abilities to build something amazing. You've done well with the gifts you've been given... but you need to always remember that they're gifts from God.

My father-in-law became a quadriplegic after an accident he had while working as a carpenter. One morning, he asked, "How'd you sleep, Chris?" I said, "I slept alright, but my back hurts." He looked at me and said, "I can only imagine."

In life, it's so easy to find things to complain about and to look at what we wish was different...But there will always be someone who has it worse than you.

It's hard to be generosity-driven if you're not grateful for what you have because you'll always be chasing more. Without gratitude, you're in "lack," and it's hard to be generous when you feel like you don't have enough.

In the book of 1 Thessalonians, Paul tells us to "in everything give thanks." The beginning of gratitude is the discipline of saying, "I will decide to no longer consume myself with the pursuit of more."

I think we need to get rid of Thanksgiving Day and make it "Grumbling Day." 364 days out of the year, we grumble and complain about what we don't have, and on one day we sit down to eat a meal with our family and give thanks. Shouldn't this be the other way around? Shouldn't we give thanks every day?

Our focus on complaining over gratitude is something humans have done for thousands of years...

Let's look at this passage from the Old Testament: "And they journeyed from Mount Hor by the way of the Red Sea, to compass the land of Edom: and the soul of the people was much discouraged because of the way. And the people spake against God, and against Moses, Wherefore have ye brought us up out of Egypt to die in the wilderness? for there is no bread, neither is there any water; and our soul loatheth this light bread." (Nu 21:4–5).

God's people had forgotten what he had brought them out of. They had gotten tired, and instead of being grateful that he delivered them from Egypt, they complained. Before, they had been slaves in Egypt and beaten, and forced to work, and their children were killed if they were born male. Now, they are free! God gives them water from a rock and angel food in the form of manna falls from heaven to feed them every day. They should be praising God and giving thanks for all that he has given them... But they are complaining.

How often do we complain because we forget what he brought us from? We focus on what we don't have rather than on how far we have come.

When we change our perspective to a perspective of thanksgiving...of gratitude, it begins to loosen the chains of the love of money and allows us to be generous.

CHAPTER 5

Generosity

To understand generosity, you need to know generous people.

You might be thinking, "Well, I don't know many generous people."

It's your lucky day—I'm about to introduce you to one.

"For God so loved the world that he gave his only begotten son, that whosoever believeth in him should not perish, but have everlasting." (John 3:16)

There was one generous person who gave up everything he had as the King of Kings to be born of a virgin, grow up in a humble carpenter's family, and die on a cross to save us all from our sins.

If that's not generosity, I don't know what is.

Philippians 2:6-8 says, "Who, being in very nature God, did not consider equality with God something to be used to his own advantage; rather he made himself nothing by taking the very nature of a servant, being made in human likeness. And being found in appearance as a man, he humbled himself by becoming obedient to death."

When we reflect on what Jesus did for us, not just in the crucifixion, but in the mere act of being born a man, it changes our view of generosity because that is the most generous act ever.

What Do You Love?

Henry Ward Beecher said, *"Watch, lest prosperity destroy generosity."*

When we're ruled by the love of money, our prosperity can destroy our generosity and set us on a never-ending quest for "more."

Through gratitude, we disconnect from our love for money. But guess what? Love always looks for somewhere else to attach itself. Attach your love to God, and when you do, you will love the things that he does.

Generosity can only happen as we redirect our love. Instead of being ruled by the love of money, or the love of things, all of a sudden we love the people and the causes that God loves.

William Booth, the founder of the Salvation Army, was on his deathbed and not able to make it to the Salvation Army's annual gathering. They asked him to send a telegraph with what he would like to be read.

William Booth, the founder of the Salvation Army, sends a single word: "Others." This was no ordinary message; it was a resounding call to arms, a manifesto etched in simplicity yet laden with profound significance. In one word, Booth encapsulated the very heartbeat of his mission–to prioritize others above oneself. The word reverberates with sacrificial love and a radical commitment to serve those on the fringes of society. It's as if, in that moment, Booth ignited a revolutionary spark that would blaze into a movement dedicated to the relentless pursuit of others, a legacy that continues to shape the world with compassion and selflessness. Booth didn't just send a message; he launched a symphony of transformative action, a rallying cry that would inspire generations to live a life beyond themselves.

As we disconnect from the love of money, we're able to put others first and become better disciples of God.

The Impact of Generosity...On You

A few years ago, a pastor friend joined the national trend of a "reverse offering." During the offering, there were envelopes with money inside. Members of the church were asked to grab an envelope. He said, "I want you to take this money and use it to do something generous for someone else." The next Sunday, he asked the congregation about how it felt to be generous. Everyone was electrified—they were excited about what they'd been able to do. He said, "This week, I want you to ask God to show you someone you can be generous to with your own money." People were thrilled to go out into the world and give.

I've never met a generous person who wasn't happy. When you're no longer focused on "more," you become content. Generous people understand that their money wasn't given to them. It was given to impact others. Meanwhile, Scrooge wasn't happy because he had wealth but only thought of himself...

Generosity isn't about what the gift does to the recipient, it's what it does to you when you give. The game changer is not the need that is filled. The game changer is becoming a generosity-driven person. When you're generosity-driven, you're no longer thinking about yourself, and you become happy because you're thinking about serving God and others.

The Stages of Generosity

At every stage of wealth, we live with open hands. Be generous with what you have in your hand, and God will fill your hand.

If you don't have much money, I still want you to be generosity-driven. We cannot give what we do not have. As God prospers you with your wealth, he also prospers you for generosity.

When you make $20,000 a year, generous for you might look like $15. But giving $15 might impact you in the same way that giving $1.5 million would impact someone else. And generosity isn't always about money. You can be generous with your time or talent and help others in a way that doesn't require a financial gift.

Generosity doesn't have much to do with the need. We are conduits for God's provision, and no needs scare him because his bank account can handle it all. Generosity is not about need but a heart for God, the ultimate giver.

All generosity requires sacrifice. The sacrifice looks different for everyone. If you're early in your career and not making much money, you might reduce your Starbucks intake from every morning to once a week and use that $20 you saved to help someone in need. If you're a multimillionaire with a decades-long career as a successful business owner, your version of sacrifice might be giving up a million dollars per year in excess income to give to charity. If it doesn't require sacrifice, it's not true generosity.

Luke 16:10 says, "He that is faithful in that which is least is faithful also in much: and he that is unjust in the least is unjust also in much. If therefore, ye have not been faithful in the unrighteous mammon, who will commit to your trust the true riches?" Everyone wants to be generous "one day." They say, "Don't worry, God, if I ever win the lottery, I'll donate a million dollars to the church." When people make these claims, I know that I could take one look at their giving records to see if that's true or not. If you haven't learned to give when you've had little, how will you be able to give when you have much?

There's a passage in Scripture that talks about how God knew the price and paid it. The price was the death of his son, but he willingly gave him and spared not (Romans 8:32). Have you ever been to a clothing store at the mall, seen a shirt on the rack, and thought, "That's my shirt!" Then, when you look at the price tag, you think, "Never mind, that's someone else's shirt." That's sticker shock. When Jesus looked at what it was going to cost for the salvation of mankind, there was no sticker shock. He was willing to pay the price.

Generosity is when we look at something and say, "Doing this is going to hurt, but I'm willing to make the sacrifice because what I'm doing has more value than not doing it."

We think that generosity is the amount of money on the check, but generosity isn't an amount, it's a mindset. I've had clients tell me, "Do you realize I've given $5 million away?" Congratulations, I'm glad you've given $5 million away. But remember the story in the Bible about the poor widow who gave two coins to the temple? Jesus said she gave more than anybody because she gave all she had.

God never asked us to do anything but use what's in our hands. When God calls Moses to free the people of Israel, Moses says, "God, I don't know if I can do it." God says, "What do you have in your hand?" Moses says, "I have a staff." God says, "Use what you have in your hand."

God never asks us to give what we don't possess. God doesn't say, "I need you to give $10 million to an orphanage tomorrow," if he knows you don't have $10 million. He only asks for what's in our hands.

When Jesus was standing before a hungry crowd with only five loaves and two fish, he didn't say, "If we only had more, I would be able to give." He said, "What's in your hands?" It was five loaves and two fish, so that's what he used. Everyone thinks this story is about feeding a multitude, but the point isn't what was accomplished. It was the generosity. If God wanted to feed the crowd, he could have made Manna fall from heaven, but if he did, the disciples wouldn't have witnessed a powerful lesson about generosity and they wouldn't have known the joy of being part of the miracle.

God doesn't need what we have in our hands, but we need to give what we have in our hands to understand the greatness of what he can do with open hands and a generous heart.

Your generosity is a way for you to use your success to connect with God. When your love goes from the love of money and success to the love of God, you begin to love things you never thought you would love.

When you love someone, you love what they love. I could tell you more than you'd ever want to know about baking cakes. And I don't even like cake that much... But my wife loves baking cakes, so because I love her, I'll sit down with her and watch every cake-baking show on the planet.

When we love money, we're going to love what it produces. But when we love God, we love what God loves.

CHAPTER 6

The "Click"

When I take people through the process of creating a generosity plan, I often tell them, "I want you to give $50 away this week. I want you to pray about it and ask God to show you who to give this money to. And I want you to enjoy it... I'll give you a money-back guarantee if you don't feel like you are a better person because of it. If you're not happy that you did it, come back and I'll write you a check for $50."

Guess how many checks I've had to write? Zero.

It starts with $50, but it becomes addictive when you realize how much it impacts you and those you are able to give to... And when you realize it's not your money you're giving away...

The reason we have a problem giving money away is because we think it's ours. That's the difference between stewardship and ownership.

When you think it's your money you're giving away, you think, "Oh, man, I don't want to give away what's mine." But when you understand that all you're doing is giving away the money that God has given to you, it changes everything. You start to think, "This isn't my money anyway. Let me just give some of it away in a way that I think would honor him."

All believers need to recognize that all we have comes from God, and when we give to God it comes from what he gave us. So being generous also means recognizing God's hand in my life. (1 Chronicles 29:14)

It's easy to get confused and think that you should give so that God gives blessings to you in return. From the outside, the mechanics look the same. You give, and you get something from God in return. This may happen when you begin to give. I've seen clients become more successful after becoming generous. But if you're becoming generous so that you can be more successful, you're still chained to a love of money.

This isn't the prosperity gospel that says, "Hey, give to me so I can give back to you." It is you saying, "God, this is your money, and I want to honor you in how it is used. Do with it what you desire. With this attitude, God loves to give more, but it is about the internal attitude."

The "prosperity gospel" screams, "I know you love money. Keep loving money, and you'll get more of it when you love God."

But when you love God, you'll love giving. You may find that God rewards you with blessings, but these are the byproducts of giving, not the purpose of it.

From the outside, the result might look the same, but giving out of a love of money feels empty.

> *Imagine Michael Jordan in 1995, dribbling a basketball, looking at you and saying, "Want to test me? Let's play ball and see if I'm the best player or not." I don't care how much hooping you've done—you're not going to beat Michael Jordan in 1995.*

God is to giving what Michael Jordan is to basketball and so much more. God is the all-time world champ at giving. God is looking at you going, "You want to test me? Play around and see what happens when you give. Go for it. Put me to the test." In Malachi 3:10, he said, "Bring ye all the tithes into the storehouse, that there may be meat in mine house, and prove me now herewith, saith the Lord of hosts, if I will not open you the windows of heaven, and pour you out a blessing, that there shall not be room enough to receive it." The result is the blessing of God on your life.

The prosperity gospel is driven by the love of money, but generosity is driven by a love of God. When you love God, you love the things that God loves, and you want to see his purposes fulfilled.

When God sees that you love him and will use your money to further his purposes, he tends to make more money appear for you to steward. I've seen client after client say after becoming generosity-driven, "Man, how did I end up with all this money? What's happening?" What's happening is that God is up in heaven smirking, thinking, "I can tell you exactly what happened, son. You put me to the test, and guess what? I'll pass it every single time."

The wise man said that he that scatters or gives increases, and the tightwad, or the one who holds on to his money more than he needs to, leans towards losing what he has. The giver prospers. In many ways, giving brings God's power into operation in your life. He is a giver, and he loves our giving. (Proverbs 11:24–25)

The Power of Generosity

On one missionary trip to Peru, a businessman told me, "Hey, Chris, I brought $50,000 to give away while I'm here. I need you to help me figure out where the money should go."

At the end of each day, when we were exhausted from working, we would sit down together to hang out, and I'd tell him what needs I'd heard of that day. "There's a need for $5,000 for a tin roof for the church. Right now they have a grass mat roof, so when it rains, it's impossible for the church to meet." It became our favorite part of the day to figure out what needs we could fulfill that day using his money.

A client who began living a life of generosity owned many houses, and when he turned 60, he decided he didn't want to own them anymore. All of his houses sold for at least 1.4 times what the market value was. He didn't even try to do that—it just happened. He ended up with $600,000 extra. I bet that God saw this man's generosity and thought, "I see that you love the things I love. You're sending money to the places I want money to go. You're a great conduit. Let me send you more... I know that you'll use it to do good instead of squandering it away."

A missionary came through our church, and we were set to give him a customary $150. But a young man involved with the church came to me and said, "Chris, I think God is telling me to give this guy $300." I said, "Don't get caught up in the emotions of this decision. If this is what God wants you to do, then do it." When he looked at his bank account, the excess was $312, so he gave the missionary $312. The next week, his boss calls him into the office and says, "I know you haven't asked for a raise, but I want to give you one." He got a $700-a-month raise, which was a lot for him at the time. This young man decided to give the missionary $300 a month.

Back in the day, my wife, a talented concert pianist and singer, inspired me to record a tape of her captivating performances. Filled with enthusiasm and a vision, I turned to God, expressing my intent to use the proceeds from the tape to purchase a radio station in Peru. For about a year, the tape sales accumulated, and I managed to save around $13,000.

Then, a call from my dad in Peru brought a wave of disappointment. He informed me that acquiring a radio station there required a significant investment—no less than $300,000. The enormity of the sum left me disheartened; the dream seemed unattainable.

However, providence took an unexpected turn when my dad later informed me of an opportunity. A gentleman was selling a combined radio and TV station for $35,000. Seeing potential in this prospect, my dad confidently declared, "We're going to buy it."

I hesitated, "Dad, it took me a year to save $13,000. How in the world am I going to purchase a $35,000 TV and radio station?"

In a divine orchestration, a generous man, unaware of the station's cost, reached out, expressing his intention to contribute.

I assumed it would be a $500 donation, which was a significant sum for me to receive at that time, but would be inadequate when faced with the large cost of the station.

I contacted our mission board, urging them to disclose the donation amount as soon as it arrived. A week later, the news came—$35,000.

Baffled and grateful, I called the donor, inquiring, "How did you know the station's cost?"

His response was profound, "**I didn't**." He explained that as he was about to mail a check for a smaller amount, the Holy Spirit guided him to write a check for a bigger number. This happened three times until he arrived at the number $35,000 and knew this was the amount that the Holy Spirit needed him to send.

Empowered by this unexpected provision, my dad encouraged me to take the next step—getting the station on the air. I responded, "What do you mean? Turn it on."

It turned out that it would take more than that...

While we had secured the license, an additional $23,000 was needed for equipment. With $13,000 in hand, I attended church the following Sunday, where the Lord blessed me with $10,000 in donations. The journey culminated in the establishment of the third-largest TV station in a city of 1.5 million people, a testament to the transformative power of people's generosity and God's unwavering guidance. God wanted me to use the station to spread his gospel, so all I had to do was trust in his plan and in the generosity of others.

Let me share another story about faith, dreams, and a friend named Paul. Back when I was 18 and a junior in college, I became a pastor at a small church in Arequipa, Peru. We were dreaming big, praying for money to buy some church property, and we had started saving up.

Now, my buddy Paul Forsyth was no stranger to our church. He had this dream of owning a tractor, always imagining himself sitting on the one he wanted. Paul had saved up $5,000 for his dream tractor, and he was ready to make it happen.

One day, out of the blue, Paul gave me a call. He said, "Hey, I was planning on buying a tractor for myself, but I felt like God wanted me to send it to Peru for you to use at Lighthouse Baptist Church. Make sure it plows well." Now, that's generosity right there!

And you know what? His act of kindness has been a blessing for many generations of folks in that city. Lighthouse Baptist

Church is still thriving, all thanks to Paul's generosity. Sometimes, dreams have a way of turning into something even more amazing when we share them with others.

In 1 Kings Chapter 17, during a drought, God sends Elijah to a widow who will supply him with food.

When Elijah arrives at the town gate, he sees the widow gathering sticks. He calls out to her, as God instructed, and asks for bread and water.

The woman responds in despair that she doesn't have bread—all she has is a small amount of flour and olive oil that she is going to use to make a meal for herself and her son.

Elijah says, "Don't be afraid. Make a small loaf of bread for me from what you have, then make something for you and your son. God will fill your jar of flour and jug of oil." The woman makes bread for Elijah, and miraculously, she doesn't run out of flour and oil.

Imagine the courage that it took for this poor woman to give her last bit of food to a stranger—and the courage that it took for Elijah to trust in God's instructions and ask this widow to make such a sacrifice for him.

Yet both Elijah and the widow trusted in God, and they were rewarded with a miracle... The woman made enough bread for all three people despite not having enough oil and flour to do so. Her generosity opened the windows of heaven to feed her until the famine ended.

When you follow God's directions and give where he calls you to give, he'll ensure you have enough.

As you learn to put God first and obey him, you will see him do great things. He will give you testimony after testimony of his greatness.

CHAPTER 7

Be Careful, Your Values Are Showing

I've never met anyone who didn't want to be generous...in the future.

That reminds me of a story that we often used in Peru as a preaching illustration. Two friends were sitting together getting drunk. They were talking about how good of friends they were to each other. As they talked, one friend said, "You know, I see our friendship is so real. We share everything, right?". The buddy agreed. So the friend said, "Well, if you had 1,000 horses, would you give me half?" He drunkenly said, "You know, I would."

"What about if you had 500 cows? Would you give me half?" His buddy said, "Of course, we're such good friends."

"What about if you had 200 sheep?" "Oh stop, you know I would."

Then the friend said, "Well, what about if you had two pigs? Would you give me one?" His buddy said, "Whoa now, you know that I have two pigs. That is not fair…"

The heart wants to be generous tomorrow, but when faced with personal sacrifices today, we hesitate to let go of what we have.

Future generosity is easy. Generosity today costs a lot, so we tend to avoid it. It will cost your time, money, and talents.

We all hear stories of football players getting recruited to colleges, saying, "When I make it big, I want to buy a house for my mom." Yet many of these young men wouldn't help their mom with the laundry if her life depended on it… Being generous when we get a big payday sounds glamorous, but giving what we can now requires sacrifice.

Aligning Values & Money

Real financial planning is when we align your values and your money. Many people think of this in terms of the future, as in, "Oh, in my estate plan, I'll leave some money to the children's hospital after I die." But if I were to look at your checkbook today, what would your values say that you believe in?

To make sure that your values and money align in the future, my job is to take you from where you're at now to where you're going to be in the future.

I'm not the defender of an outdated map. I'm a guide in a changing landscape. And as we navigate through this landscape, we have to make sure that your values are reflected today as well.

What values do you aspire to? Rather than envisioning a future where you practice those values, what if you practiced them today?

You think you'll be generous when you have that big payday, but **big paydays usually don't come**. People love to claim, "When I win the lottery, I'll buy the church a new building," yet they don't even fumble for their wallet when the collection basket comes around. Most of us won't have a big payday. Our income throughout life follows a trend line, making steady increases as our business grows or as we climb the ranks in our careers. We become a little bit better off in small, incremental steps. If we don't set a margin for how much is "enough" and how much is excess for giving, we won't give.

We need to have open hands and a generous heart today. If you're making minimum wage, I want you to be generous. If you're making $500 an hour, I want you to be generous. Generosity isn't about the size of the check. It's about the condition of the heart. Generosity isn't an amount, it is a mindset.

Goals are not values...values are values. Our goals should be aligned with our values, and achieving them should bring us closer to living in alignment with our values.

The values you want to hold in the future should dictate the portfolio you have today.

What do you want your eulogy to say? You're standing at your funeral—what do you hear your loved ones say about you? Write it out. These are the values you should be working toward your whole life.

I take my new clients through this exercise so that building their portfolio is working backward from the values they want to be remembered for. Here's my own eulogy in case you need inspiration for writing yours:

> *Ladies and gentlemen, friends and family, as we celebrate the life of Chris Gardner today, let us not only remember the incredible man he was but also take solace in the knowledge that he knew where he was going when he left this earthly realm. Chris's unwavering faith was the compass that guided his journey, and he would want each one of you to share in the assurance of that destination.*
>
> *Chris's investment in others was not a mere aspect of his character; it was the essence of who he was. His generosity wasn't confined to his family or close friends; it extended to anyone in need. He would give the shirt off his back to help those facing challenges, a testament to a heart that beat in rhythm with compassion. Chris understood the true meaning of giving, often leaving behind a trail of kindness and support, and he gave more than he ever took.*
>
> *In every interaction, whether it was a shared moment at home or a collaborative effort in the workplace,*

Chris lived out a philosophy of selflessness. His legacy isn't just about the material gifts he shared; it's about the countless lives he touched with his kindness, empathy, and genuine care.

So, as we bid farewell to Chris Gardner, let us carry forward the echoes of his love and generosity. Let us embody the priorities that defined him—faith, family, and a relentless commitment to others. Chris's journey may have reached its earthly conclusion, but the impact of his love will continue to resonate in our lives. May his memory inspire us to give generously, love unconditionally, and, above all, embrace the certainty of the destination that awaits each of us.

I would love to say that I live daily working towards making this goal a reality. Having such a goal helps you strive to live a life of significance. It is so easy to get caught up in daily drudgery that we lose sight of God's purpose for our lives.

Do Your Actions Match Your Values?

Your actions always match your values, but it might wake you up if you realize what that means.

There's not a single human being alive that does not want six-pack abs. And there's not one human being alive that doesn't know what they need to do to get six-pack abs. Yet there are very few human beings who actually have six-pack abs. If we know what we want and how to get it, why don't we get it?

In life, knowing how to get what you want usually isn't the issue... The problem is behavior. If you want six-pack abs, you know that you need to eat healthy and work out. But it requires discipline to eat healthy and work out daily.

It's the same with financial goals... You know how to align your values and your money, but the trouble is actually having the courage and discipline to do it. **If everyone did what they knew they should do, the world would be full of six-pack abs and billionaires**.

Are your actions aligned with what you say your values are? If you say you value generosity, but you never give, how much do you really value generosity?

A great financial professional should help you align your actions with your values. Every financial decision you make should be made with the intention of bringing you closer to your values. If you value generosity, your financial decisions should help you be more generous.

Yet most traditional financial planners focus on creating "more" money without any clue why having more money matters to the client. These planners base a client's plan on what the market is doing.

But your values matter more than the market. Your investments exist to support your values.

As a result, we don't change your plan based on what the market is doing... We change your plan when your values change. As long as your plan allows you to live the life you want to live, aligned with your values, you don't need to worry about whether the market is up or down today.

When we align your plan with your values, you no longer have to fear shifts in the market. As long as we're able to accomplish your goals and live up to your values, your portfolio will serve its purpose.

You also need to make sure your generosity aligns with your values. With thousands of charitable organizations in the world, it can be difficult to determine where to allocate your money to have the greatest impact on causes that matter to you. Working with a philanthropic strategist can help you get clarity and align your giving to your values.

CHAPTER 8

—————/\—————

Building Your Giving Strategy

"For we are his workmanship, created in Christ Jesus unto good works, which God hath before ordained that we should walk in them."

–Ephesians 2:10

Mark 14:7 says, "For ye have the poor with you always."

There will always be needs. No amount of money fixes the human condition. We could bring Bill Gates, Jeff Bezos, Elon Musk, and Warren Buffett into a room, have them empty all of their bank accounts, and still not have enough money to solve every problem in the world. Even if it could, it would only take a day for new needs to pop up. Because of that, we have to be strategic in the way that we give money.

God has given you an innate desire to impact certain spheres of influence. He's given you things you're passionate about, things you like, things you want to change, things in the world that bother you, and things you think you can have an impact on.

The amount of need in the world is so gigantic that generosity will never fix it, so you have to tailor your generosity to what God has placed in your heart and made you want to be a part of.

When making your generosity plan, we'll uncover what you're passionate about, and then we'll research ways to make an impact in that area.

But generosity isn't about handing out money to some organization and then sitting back while others make an impact. Generosity is about more than money... Ideally, you'll become actively involved in the issue you're passionate about, and money is just one facet of that.

It's easy to fall into the trap of thinking our abundance in material wealth gives us a free ride, exempting us from investing any other facet of our lives into the very things God has laid on our hearts. Let me tell you, a fat checkbook is no substitute for what a dirty hand and a heart brimming with generosity can do for others when we give them our time. Checkbooks are cold, but our time is bold. Money may be necessary, but it's our time that carries the real weight. Make intentional choices about where you sow your financial seeds, but don't forget to deliberate just as wisely about where you invest the precious currency of your time.

A generosity plan ensures that we don't follow needs, we follow our vision. Focus brings success. Needs are always there, but if our focus is scattered we may not send our money to where it can have the most impact. Giving in accordance with a plan helps you make change in the world that aligns with your values and God's plan for you.

What unique dent do you want to make in the world? What 3-5 issues are you passionate about? What is your mission? What is your vision?

Once you unpack what those are, it's helpful to have a "dreaming partner" who is experienced in giving, can help you talk through your giving plans, and connect you with people who can inform you about how to help.

Being a "dreaming partner" for my clients is one of the great privileges of my life, and it is one of the things I enjoy doing most in the world. As someone who has been on both sides of the table of generosity, both a recipient and a giver, witnessing others discover the power of giving is an incredible, awe-inspiring experience.

There are an infinite number of needs and an infinite number of ways to help. The sheer size and scale of that can be overwhelming. A thinking partner can help you clarify your generosity plan and remain focused on your mission. A good thinking partner will always have an eye for what your next steps are and will keep you on track. A great professional will understand this and help with this as much as with the investment side of things.

Giving For Impact

A generosity plan is crucial because if you hand out your money poorly, you can create more problems for the recipient of your gift.

> An American missionary abroad couldn't get people to come to church, so he offered them rice and beans for coming. But when he went back to the United States and turned the church back over to the local preacher, the local preacher got accused of stealing all the rice and beans for himself. The missionary's seemingly smart and noble plan to lure people to church with the free rice and beans backfired... They had started going to the church expecting to receive free food rather than going because they wanted to worship. They'd become dependent on the handouts from the missionary, and they were angry when these handouts stopped. It took years for this church community to recover from the incident and have an impact in the community because the locals believed that the preacher was stealing the rice and beans from his people. This situation may seem unthinkable, but the truth is that, many times, the way we give money to needs and organizations mirrors this.

A common problem that arises with missionaries is that they give a gift that can't be sustained.

For example, let's say a missionary builds a church in a poor community in Africa. He builds an American church because that's his only frame of reference. Meaning he installs a projector, prints bulletins every week, and buys nice instruments for a worship band... But when he returns to America, the church won't be able to sustain these expenses. If a bulb goes out in the projector, they won't be able to replace it. I encourage missionaries to think about what will happen when they leave, not just what happens when they're there. It's not a bad thing to help buy a church, but if you want your gift to have a lasting impact, you need to give in a way that the community will be able to sustain when you walk away.

I often encourage givers to make sure that the recipient can afford 10-20% of the goal. If a church needs a new building, they should be able to afford 10-20% of the building and accept donations to cover the rest. If the church can't cover that much, they may be dreaming outside of their wheelhouse, and the new building may be an unsustainable expense after the donors walk away. Think about the size of house you might want if money wasn't an issue. The limits that money places on you help guide you in ways that keep your spending reasonable and sustainable.

> *"Don't write a check from a distance thinking you have done your part."*
>
> **–Carl Richards**

Anyone who's built a business knows that the business was built in struggle. Without the struggle, you would not be where you are today. The journey built the business, not money. What would have happened if someone walked in the second week your business was open and gave you $3 million? You would be happy to have that $3 million, but the business would not be where it is today because you missed out on the journey that taught you important lessons. The struggle helps you grow so that you can succeed.

Things that grow because of money die because of money. Luke 14:28-29 says on this topic, "For which of you, intending to build a tower, sitteth not down first, and counteth the cost, whether he have sufficient to finish it? Lest haply, after he hath laid the foundation, and is not able to finish it, all that behold it begin to mock him."

If you give $3 million to an organization that isn't equipped to handle $3 million, that money may not have the impact you thought it would. Like a business, this organization needs to grow and scale at a steady rate over time. For example, maybe a small religious school starts with a handful of students. $2,000 a month may be enough to support these students. But as the school grows, attracts more students, accumulates more needs, and discovers more opportunities to do good, they become equipped to handle larger donations. But if you just handed this small school a check for $1 million, it may overwhelm them and hold back their ability to grow.

If you give in an unsustainable way, your gift may die when you die. For example, if you found an orphanage through a one-time, lump-sum gift of $3 million, the orphanage is at risk of closing when the $3 million runs out, and if you've passed away, you won't be able to give them more money. This doesn't mean that your gift was bad–you've still done good in the world–but if you gave in a more strategic, ongoing way, you could do more good in the world and increase the impact of your gift.

The Fallacy of Full-Time Ministry

Most people believe that because pastors get paid, they're the only ones in full-time ministry while the rest of us aren't. Want to see if you're in full-time ministry or not? We can use the two-finger test again.

Do you have a pulse? Are you a Christian?

Congratulations, you're in full-time ministry. If God has saved you, you're in full-time ministry. No matter what your profession is, the expectations on your pastor are no different from the expectations on you. You just carry out your ministry in a different realm. The job of every follower of Christ is to be the salt and the light. But today, too many people practice "salt shaker Christianity." Salt doesn't lose its flavor— unless it stays in the salt shaker. People say, "My salt shaker is better than yours. My church is better than your church. My thoughts are better than your thoughts."

Meanwhile, the salt stays in the shaker rather than being dispersed to the community that it's supposed to impact. We're supposed to add flavor to life, but we don't. We stay in the salt shaker and call it holiness. That's not holiness. That's you not doing what God has called you to do. Get out of the salt shaker and impact the world.

But a word of caution... We are not generous because of the tax benefits. We're generous because we're generous. When God leads us to do something, we do it whether there's a tax benefit or not. But if there happens to be a tax benefit, why would we not use it? Leveraging a tax benefit is good stewardship of what God has given you. It can extend your impact by leaving you with more to give. But don't go looking for tax benefits or let them limit who you give to... That's the love of money taking over. We seek to turn taxable dollars into charitable dollars.

You can invest the money in different instruments and grow the amount of money you're able to give. In other words, you can give the milk from the cow, not the steak from the cow.

If you have $10 million that you want to give away, deciding how to give it can be overwhelming. But there are financial instruments where you can set that money aside for charity and then decide over time how to distribute it. As you discover needs that align with your mission, you can use a little of the money at a time.

Having the right strategy matters... There are many different financial instruments that can multiply your generosity. Having an advisor that understands these tools is vital. The only way to know which strategy is best for you is to talk to an advisor and get an assessment of your unique situation.

It's important to define what success looks like for your generosity plan. How will you know you're making an impact? Having a goal for what you want your money to do for the world helps us decide how to best allocate it. If we find that a certain organization isn't producing the impact that you're targeting, we want to research other organizations and find one that will.

Generosity that is only given when needs arise will not bring that fulfillment you are looking for. When you have a strategy for your generosity, you will know what to say no to. Saying no is a viable option... It means that you'll have more to give when you say yes to the right person... The person God has called you to give to.

CHAPTER 9

Your Continuing Problem

The problem with many financial advisors is that they shoot for this ideal called "retirement," which means you'll be put out of service. But that's not an ideal for a person with a serious drive given to you by God. If you tell most of my clients, "You can sit in your recliner seven days a week and do nothing," they'd say, "Do I have to?" It almost feels like they are trying to put us out to pasture.

Driven people don't usually ever want to retire, so let's put that word to the side and start asking ourselves about rewiring instead of retiring.

A counselor has done well and saved well, so he decides to work a little longer but is now giving 60% of his time to counsel and coach people in full-time ministry. He has given himself the freedom to do this by saving well and preparing, and this has enabled him to repurpose his life.

Retirement isn't always the goal. Financial planning for retirement simply means we're going to build you a safety net so that if your health declines in old age, you're no longer reliant on the income from your career or business to live on. We want to make sure you can always pass the "bus test" (what would happen if you got hit by a bus tomorrow?). If the worst-case scenario happens to you, whether that means becoming physically or mentally incapacitated or dying, we want to make sure you can still provide for those you love. This doesn't mean you have to give up living an active, ambitious lifestyle if you don't want to.

As a matter of fact, most of my clients have no desire to have a *normal* retirement.

If you're not shooting for "retirement," you'll have an ongoing problem—you'll continue to be successful and create wealth. So what do you do with all of the excess wealth that you create?

You need a financial advisor who will help you formulate an ongoing plan for giving once you reach your finish line.

Your finish line is the amount of money you decided would be your income to live on. There are two finish lines that really matter: the lifestyle finish line, which is what you will live on every month, and the lifetime finish line, which is the amount you will pursue for retirement or rewiring.

After we reach the finish line, we run into the danger of collecting paper instead of pursuing purpose.

People can't see the picture because they're in it. A financial advisor's job is to look at the picture and say, "Let me tell you what you can't see." We all have blind spots. I don't care how smart you are, we all have blind spots. It's helpful to bring in an expert who shows you those blind spots and then helps you.

Building Your Generosity Plan

Though your exact "finish line" needs to be assessed by an advisor, a rule of thumb to give you an idea is 33 times what you want for your total annual spending. If you want to spend $100,000 in a year, your finish line for retirement will be $3.3 million. This is "enough." Saving up beyond $3.3 million makes little sense.

After you've saved the amount you need for retirement, you'll set aside what you want to leave for your family. If you passed away, how much would your spouse need to live on? How much do you want to leave to your kids? If you have saved 33 times, then the original amount is approximately what you will also leave behind, not counting anything extra.

"If I'm interviewing your children in 30 years and I ask them about their relationship with money, and you are listening to the interview, what do you hope they are saying about their relationship with money?"

–Carl Richard

"I hope my children say that they learned to not be afraid of money and that they learned to make choices being informed by money but not governed by it."

–Caroline Randall Williams

And after you've reached your "finish line" for yourself and your family, what will you do with the excess? And why don't we start that now?

Think of it like filling buckets with water. We fill your bucket of retirement savings to prepare for tomorrow. Then, we fill your family legacy bucket. But after these two buckets are full, the water begins to overflow. Your wealth doesn't stop growing once you fill these two buckets. What will you do with the rest? Will you just give the government a good tip after you're gone? I love leaving a good tip for a waiter, but I can't stand the thought of leaving a tip for the government. This is where your generosity plan comes in. Your strategy for giving will become more complex as your wealth grows in time.

The Typical Financial Advisor Annual Review vs. The Annual Generosity Review

This is what an annual review with a typical financial planner looks like: "Your portfolio looks good. This is how much return you've had. You're still on target. Anything I can help you with? Okay, have a great day, and talk to you next year."

That annual review is important, but it does nothing to address a person's values.

But when you work with an advisor to create a generosity plan, that annual review could be, "You're free to give another $350,000 this year because everything is working the way we planned it." This is much more fun and energizing than just looking at numbers that don't mean anything to you.

Financial planning is not just about the numbers. It's about what these numbers mean. It's about helping people live out their values and become generous with the wealth they've built.

Look for a financial advisor who prioritizes values over numbers.

As I mentioned earlier in the book, the three phases of wealth are:

1. You get to the point where you produce more than you consume. In your younger years, when you're starting in your career, you need to get to the point where you're making more money than you need to live on each month so you can pay your bills and put food on the table without worrying that you won't have enough money to cover your basic needs.
2. You get to the point where you produce more than you *will* consume—meaning you have lifetime savings set aside for retirement or repurposing of your life.
3. You produce so you can reproduce... With both your daily needs and your retirement savings provided for, you focus on growing your money so that it generates wealth that you can use to fulfill your purpose.

Without a giving plan, when you get to phase three you'll have an amazing problem—you'll have so much excess money that you don't know what to do with it. Many people at this stage end up wasting this money on worldly luxuries that don't make them happy or please God... Or they end up "collecting paper," letting this money grow just so they can feel prideful about how much they have. But when you have a giving plan, phase three allows you to become a money machine on God's behalf. You can focus on growing and reproducing money so that you can give more of it away, help more people, and make a bigger impact in the world in whatever way God has commanded you to.

It's Not About The Barn...

In the Bible, there are two contrasting stories about saving crops in barns.

In the New Testament, Jesus tells a parable about a rich man who builds a barn so that he can save his crops for many years and be prosperous. God says to him, "Thou fool, this night thy soul shall be required of thee: then whose shall those things be, which thou hast provided?" (Luke 12:16-21)

Many people misinterpret this parable, thinking it means that we should not save money or build wealth.

But Jesus finishes this story with the words, "So is he that layeth up treasure for himself, and is not rich toward God."

The problem isn't the barn... It's that the man wanted to selfishly hoard all of his wealth in the barn rather than sharing it abundantly with others. It's not inherently wrong to save money or build wealth... But it is wrong if we do so for our own benefit rather than for God's benefit.

This man thought only of himself. He thought, "I have it made. I am in good shape." It was a me, my, I story. He did not think, "What is God doing with me and why has he given me this wealth?" Remember, God gives us richly all things to enjoy, but more than that, he wants us to do good with what he gives us. He wants us to be rich, but rich in good works. He wants his people to be willing givers, always looking for the opportunity to give. In effect, he calls those that he gives money to be generous.

We can contrast this parable with the story of Joseph in the Old Testament. In the years during which food was plentiful, Joseph gathers and saves food in a barn. Then, in the famine years, Joseph is able to feed the people of Israel with what he saved.

If Joseph hadn't saved, his people would have starved... There's nothing wrong with saving. Saving helps us prepare for emergencies and weather difficult times. But saving dishonors God if we make it about hoarding wealth and loving money.

Money is a tool that we can use to accomplish God's mission for us. It's good stewardship of our money to save and invest wisely so that we have more resources to help others... But if we behave like the rich fool, building wealth so we can greedily keep it for ourselves, we are disobeying God's will.

Wealth isn't the problem—our attitude towards it is. What's your attitude towards wealth? Are we building wealth for ourselves, out of a love of money? Or are we building wealth so that we can share it with others and accomplish God's purpose for us?

We need to live our lives with purpose and fulfill the unique missions that God has given each of us to accomplish his will on earth.

The solution to our continuing problem of "What do I do with all of this excess money?" is to align our wealth with God's purpose for us.

Go out and do good with your God-given resources. Be rich, yes, but be rich in doing good works. Don't wait until there is a need. Be a willing giver who seeks opportunities to give. Be a worthy steward of God's money. Be generosity-driven.

CHAPTER 10

A Community of Generosity

When you start out in your career or in building a business, it's a struggle and a grind for what might seem like an eternity. Then, after all that work, all of a sudden, the business starts producing cash flow.

As your wealth increases, your social circle tends to get wealthier, too. Not because you're excluding people who aren't as wealthy but simply because, as a successful person, you encounter other successful people. If you can now afford to move your family to a nicer neighborhood, your neighbors will be other successful people who can afford to live in that neighborhood. Or as you get invited to high-level networking events in your industry, you'll befriend others whose hard work has made them wealthy.

But the problem with being surrounded by wealthy and successful peers is that many of them will not use their wealth in a God-honoring way. All around you, the conversations will be focused on a love of money. "Did you see the new gadget Apple just launched?" "Are you taking any vacations this summer? My wife and I just got back from a five-star hotel in Italy, and it was amazing." "We're thinking about buying a beach house." "Look at John's new car..."

When wealthy people aren't focused on serving God, it's easy to become enamored with upgrading your lifestyle. And when you find yourself in a social group of successful people who wear Rolexes, drive Porsches, and are constantly talking about what they want to do with their money, it's easy to lose sight of God's true purpose for your wealth.

That's why it's crucial to find a community of people who embrace generosity. Instead of talking about the latest Porsche or Rolex, your generosity community will talk about how they took the money that God gave them and used it to further his kingdom. These people will encourage you on your giving journey and help you focus on what's important.

When you surround yourself with this community, you realize you're not the only crazy person in the world who wants to give away your wealth on behalf of God. When you're immersed in the dominant money-loving, success-loving culture, you may feel like you're the only crazy one who is focused on charity, not on worldly pleasures.

Alan and Katherine Barnhart are a Christian couple who are co-CEOs of Barnhart Crane & Rigging, a company based in Memphis, Tennessee with offices in forty cities across the US. When Alan's parents exited the business, leaving him as the owner when he was a young, newly married man, Alan worried that the business would be successful... It's funny, isn't that the opposite of what most people worry about? But Alan feared that affluence would stand in the way of his relationship with God. He said, "I feared that business success could be very detrimental to my life. There were dozens of verses that brought me to that conclusion. I saw it in other people's lives. It's a choice tool of our enemy. This whole thing with greed is something our enemy uses to twist us around, and that includes believers. I didn't want that to be my reality."

To combat this fear, Alan and Katherine decided that "God owns the business," and they set a "finish line" for their income. As a young couple, this finish line was $40,000, but later in life, after they'd started a family of six children, they increased this amount to $160,000 so they could afford to send their children to college. Any income beyond this finish line would be given to charity. Despite their affluence, the couple lives a simple life, giving their wealth up to God rather than pursuing the luxurious lifestyle that so many others with their level of success choose to have.

In 2019, the company's revenue was over $400 million. When the company started, the couple's first charitable gift was $50,000, and an ambitious member of the sales team suggested that they set a goal of eventually giving $1 million per month. As soon as the couple set this goal, the company boomed, and since 2005, the couple has been able to give at least $1 million a month to charity. In 2019, they gave $21 million for the year.

After the business's tremendous success, Alan and his brother, who is his business partner, decided that since God owned the company, they should give the company away. A wise advisor designed a plan for them to put the company in a trust. Alan and his family gave up ownership of the company while remaining stewards of it.

Of what she learned on her journey, Katherine Barnhart said, "God had to show me that it's not about me serving him. It's about Him. It's about the Lord glorifying himself in and through me. The paradigm shift here is that I'm not the one in control, he's the one in control. I'm not the one with the influence, he's the one with the influence. I'm not the one with the power, he's the one with the power. I'm not even the one with the resources... He's the one with the resources."

Remaining Focused on Your Generosity Mission

Now that people know you as a giver and you build more relationships with other charitable individuals, you're being pulled in 1000 directions to give. You're invited to galas and other fundraising events, and people often approach you about contributing to their organizations. Without a generosity strategy, this can be overwhelming.

I train all my clients to get comfortable saying the following phrase: "I'm sorry, that's just not what I do because I have a plan for what my generosity looks like." If you get approached to contribute money to a cause that isn't aligned with the mission you outlined in your generosity strategy, all you have to say is, "I'm sorry, that's just not what I do."

Building a Generosity Community

Who you are is dictated by the books you read, the people you hang out with, and the places you go. As you build wealth, those people become wealthy individuals who read books about how to become richer, go to nice restaurants, and brag about the latest and greatest car they bought.

You need to find people who are given to generosity more than they are given to the American dream. You need to find people who put generosity at the core of life and understand that their success is a blessing from God.

But how do you find this group of peers?

That community already exists...

It exists among our clients. We love introducing our clients to each other and hearing them talk about the amazing charitable ventures they're involved in.

There is nothing quite like getting four to five families in a room to hear them discussing how God led their families in different ways. Tears usually flow, and you can see smiles from ear to ear as each of them explains the reason for their decision, the verses God laid on their hearts, and the individual strategies that each of them has.

It is quite exciting to be the proverbial fly on the wall while one follower of Christ asks another about ways to do what they have always dreamed of doing. It is neat to hear the humility of the CEO and founder exclaiming how his company with 500 employees has been structured in one way, while another with a much smaller company explains how they decided to structure things their way.

What you learn as you are a part of these incredible meetings is that there is not one prescription that works for every company in every environment all of the time. Having strategic partners like the community we have the privilege of serving and advisors who have the same heart for God creates a synergy that is almost impossible to replicate. The good news is that we are always looking for more people with this heartbeat to add to that community.

CHAPTER 11

The Impact of Generosity... On You!

Generosity is not about others. It will impact others, but it is about you.

The Bible states that it's better to give than to receive. If you're a parent, you've seen this firsthand on Christmas. Watching your young kids open the toys you chose for them puts a smile on your face, while opening your own presents is nice but doesn't have the same effect. It's natural to want to give to your children, but imagine how much more powerful this feeling could be when you give freely to others in the world without expecting anything in return.

As we let go of the love of money through gratitude and generosity and shift our love to God's creation, we get the same joy of giving that you get when giving presents to your family on Christmas but magnified on a larger scale.

When I was 18 years old, I was the pastor of a church. A young couple who attended the church got pregnant out of wedlock, ran away from home, and were going to abort their child. The young woman's brother came to me for help, and we spent four sleepless days and nights driving around the city to find the couple. We found them, brought them home, and convinced them to have their child.

Eighteen years later, the church I had pastored was having an anniversary, so I was invited to preach for the special occasion. As I was about to leave, a young girl came up to me and said, "Can I take a selfie with you?"

We took the picture, and then she wrapped her arms around me and started sobbing. She said, "You convinced my parents not to abort me. I just wanted to say thank you."

I had held this young girl when she was born, and now she was eighteen years old. As I stood there, I realized the immensity of the gift I had given her. I had helped this young couple eighteen years ago simply because I felt it was the right thing to do, and now this young woman, their daughter, was crying and thanking me for the life she was blessed to live.

My gift had impacted her, but more than anything, it impacted me. It brought me great joy to realize that God had used me to bless this young woman with the gift of life. To the day I die, I will tell that story and feel the impact of my own generosity.

The Myth of Scarcity

I have a question for you that has the power to shape your world.

Please close your eyes and, for a few seconds, think of the two people who have most positively impacted your life...

I've asked this question at the basin of the Amazon River, in the world's largest, driest desert, and in the middle of the most urbanized landscapes, and the answers always resonate with me. No matter the language spoken or the number of translators involved, the answers always come down to one thing.

That person that came to mind for you impacted you... through their generosity.

Our view of generosity shapes who we are.

The word generosity tends to shift our minds to the changes that could be made if only... We could spend other people's money.

Isn't it funny how the easiest money to spend is always someone else's?

We've cheapened generosity by thinking that it is always tied to money.

But if you were to tell the story of your two people... I can almost guarantee that it has nothing to do with money.

You know why? Because generosity is not an amount, it's a mindset.

I was twelve when I got on my first airplane, headed on an adventure to the driest desert in the world.

This trip was different because we were missing one major thing...

We didn't have a return ticket.

My family was moving to what would become my adopted country where my best friends in the world live to this day.

Those who didn't live in Lima, the capital city at that point, were making around twenty dollars a month.

We arrived to a country in turmoil.

The media only shared the doom and gloom of the reality Peru was in, and... it made all the sense in the world to my twelve-year-old self.

There was a desperation in the air that you could almost feel.

One thing was certain: this wasn't a normal feeling for a twelve-year-old.

Especially this time of the year.

You see...

Christmas was around the corner, and instead of having conversations with my friends about what we might be getting,

I could overhear my friend's mother explaining how Christmas was the worst time of the year.

My dad had a plan that he thought could help during this time of scarcity. We would be giving away Christmas baskets to 10 families who were in even more need.

I pretty much lived in the home of my adopted family, and I was so angry that he would even think to suggest this.

See, when I was lying in bed with my friends, I overheard the parents talking quietly to each other about how they weren't sure what the family would eat the next day, and here my dad was talking about giving gifts to others.

But they were more receptive to the idea than I was...

We went home that night, and all of us now had problems going to sleep.

We couldn't stop talking about ideas of things we could make and give in these baskets.

We came up with the idea to create wooden pistols out of spare wood that we had begged carpenters to give to us.

The pistols started fairly large, but then we realized that this was going to be impossible with the small scraps that were left, so small pistols it was.

We took thrown-away condensed milk cans and, with a Sharpie, drew faces on the robots we had just fashioned out of these cans and attached them to each other with construction wire.

We spent hours planning, talking about how we could be intentionally generous in the midst of our scarcity.

My friends and I scavenged and found pieces that would become parts of our master creation.

We never got a call from Mattel® or Hasbro®, but we were so excited with the toys we made.

Christmas morning, we delivered the baskets...the joy that the recipients felt was nothing compared to our joy.

I will never forget hearing my adopted mom saying to others that this was her best Christmas ever.

What a change in perspective!

In the midst of scarcity, we had found abundance.

We knew that being generosity-driven would change our lives.

That day I learned a few things:

Generosity fulfills the giver as much as the receiver.

It creates a bond with those who are generous together.

It alters your view on generosity when you realize that it isn't always tied to money.

And the overarching truth of it all...

Generosity inspires generosity, and it is contagious!

I can always be generous with what I do have.

Being intentionally generous took my mind off what we didn't have.

I learned that day... the joy that comes from intentional generosity.

Embracing generosity liberates us from a fixation on Leaving a Legacy, and it frees us to Live a Legacy today!

My challenge to you is this... decide that every day you will be intentionally generous. Not a half-baked decision like "I want to be healthy one day," but instead say, "I will wake up every morning and find two specific people I can be generous to today."

What would the world look like if we decided that we would be intentionally generous?

Generosity has little to do with what we carry in our wallets.

What if we were intentionally generous with our time with those who need it?

What if we were intentionally generous while talking or listening to others?

What if we decided that we would be kind even to someone who didn't deserve it?

What if we were intentionally generous in our gratitude towards others?

Being generosity-driven is something we can control.

We can learn from our children.

They don't understand generosity with money, but we can teach them to be generous with their currency (toys, attention, sharing, or understanding).

When we do this, we are teaching our children to live with open hands and generous hearts.

If we teach them generosity by living generosity, then the study done by Cerulli Associates 2022 doesn't scare us as much.

This study states that through 2045, over 85 trillion dollars will be passed down.

Over 70 trillion of those dollars will be directly passed down to the children.

This is what the world I work in calls the World's Greatest Wealth Transfer!

Can you imagine the impact this kind of wealth could have on our world?

This wealth will only be seen through the eyes of generosity if we model intentional generosity to those around us today!

Here's an important truth: today's generosity shapes tomorrow's values, even when wealth arrives.

Intentional Generosity changes lives and teaches us to live life with open hands and generous hearts.

Intentional Generosity does what money cannot and can be the answer where money is not.

Can you imagine for a minute what a world that took generosity seriously might look like?

Can you imagine a world where generosity was at the core of our DNA?

Can you imagine if generosity was such a part of our DNA that it became part of our Global Education System?

Do you remember the way you felt when you were extravagantly generous?

Maybe it was on Christmas morning watching with delight the joy that your generosity brought to your loved ones!

As a child, I learned that there are very few things as powerful as generosity in the midst of scarcity, and that changed my life because I realized...

That the checks that I wrote on my generosity account would never bounce.

That means we can live like the richest people in the world.

When we shift our perspective from what we want to what we have, our lives begin to change.

You know why?

Because Generosity inspires Generosity, and it is contagious.

If you are generosity-driven, and it becomes a habit, I cannot tell you that it will change the world, but I can guarantee you that it will change someone's world...

And even more important is this... I can promise that it will change yours.

I want you to imagine a world twenty years down the road when your grandchildren gather around during Christmas time and tell the stories of who you were.

I hope my family talks about the lives that were impacted because of our generosity.

Imagine a world where we wake up in the morning and ask, "What two people will I show generosity to today?"

Yes! Intentional Generosity in the midst of scarcity is a challenge, but... an easier dent cannot be made in the world than the dent we make when we are intentionally generous.

I challenge you today to observe your environment looking for a place to be generous... but a word of caution...

Be very, very careful because if you look for places to be generous, you will find them.

Remember those two people that have impacted your life the most?

If you live with generosity as part of your DNA, someday someone might close their eyes to think of the two people that impacted their life the most and think of you.

We have no scarcity of the things in life that really matter. Let's be generosity-driven.

Conclusion

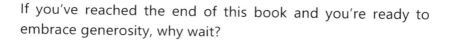

If you've reached the end of this book and you're ready to embrace generosity, why wait?

Don't spend any longer collecting paper or chasing the mirage of "more."

There are only three places your money can go:

1) **You can spend it**
2) **You can save it**
3) **You can give it**

After you've reached a certain level of comfort in life, spending your money on yourself won't make you any happier. Remember what Solomon said... "All is vanity." There's no luxury product anywhere in the world that will make you as happy as giving can.

The second option is to save your money... But after you've saved more than enough to provide for yourself and your family for the rest of your days (and to be prepared for any emergency you can imagine), saving money is just collecting paper. You don't get to take that paper with you when you leave this Earth... Looking at the number in your savings or investment accounts might make you feel proud, but this feeling is nothing compared to the joyful feeling of giving to others. Why hoard your money when the cause of Christ is of so much more value?

Giving is the only option of the three that has the power to bring true joy.

Imagine how it will feel to know that you are making an impact in the lives of others... To know that your accomplishments in your business or career are enabling you to serve others... To give hope to those in need... To share God's light with those who are in darkness...

And imagine how deeply satisfying it will be to know that you are aligned with God's purpose. No longer will you be wandering the desert, lost, searching for the fulfillment you crave. You'll be set on a course of action that will transform your life and bring you more blessings than you can even know.

Why would you wait to enjoy these incredible blessings?

God has a purpose for you, and he's waiting for you to have the courage to align yourself with it. At this very moment, he has a plan for the wealth that he has allowed you to build... Will you accept it, or will you continue down the path of worldly desire that leads you nowhere?

Commit to generosity today, and watch as God's hand guides you toward your purpose.

Next Steps

When you're ready to explore creating your own generosity plan, here are three ways I can help:

1. Go to generositydriven.com/resources for tools that will empower you in your pursuit of generosity.

2. Are you a member of an organization filled with successful, mission-driven people looking to make a difference in the world? I'd love to speak at your next conference, event, or retreat. Visit chrisgardnerspeaks.com or call 678-646-4692.

3. Want to work with me 1-on-1 to build your generosity plan, so that you're making a bigger and bigger impact with your wealth, without giving it all to the IRS? Call 678-646-4692 or email chris@generositydriven.com and mention this book.

About the Author

Chris is a financial advisor and philanthropic strategist whose remarkable journey began over two decades ago in Peru. As a missionary, he cultivated a deep connection with diverse cultures and learned to appreciate the unique stories of the individuals he met. The experience molded his approach to financial planning, making him a trusted advisor who genuinely understands the importance of aligning financial strategies with personal values.

He holds Bachelor's and Master's degrees earned during his time overseas, highlighting his commitment to comprehensive, purpose-driven financial planning. Chris is passionate about empowering his clients to pursue their passions with informed, strategic financial choices.

Together with his wife, Andria, Chris has built a beautiful family life over 28 years of marriage, raising four children and pastoring a church in Marietta, GA. Their profound connection to Peru and shared adventures add a personal touch to his professional expertise. A devoted Georgia Bulldog fan, Chris cherishes time spent with his loved ones, drawing strength and inspiration from these close relationships.

Made in the USA
Columbia, SC
06 December 2024

47453044R00078